Integrating the Digital Humanities into the Second Language Classroom

Integrating the Digital Humanities into the Second Language Classroom

A Practical Guide

Melinda A. Cro

GEORGETOWN UNIVERSITY PRESS

The publisher is not responsible for third-party websites or their content. URL links were active at time of publication.

ISBN 978-1-62616-776-6 (paperback)
ISBN 978-1-62616-777-3 (ebook)

Library of Congress Control Number: 2019950115

♾ This book is printed on acid-free paper meeting the requirements of the American National Standard for Permanence in Paper for Printed Library Materials.

21 20   9 8 7 6 5 4 3 2   First printing

Printed in the United States of America.
Cover design by Pam Pease.
Cover image courtesy of iStock by Getty Images / skynesher.

To Ryan, with love

Contents

Acknowledgments   ix

Abbreviations   xi

Introduction: How Does the Second Language Classroom
Benefit from the Digital Humanities?   1

1   The Digital Humanities: Definitions and Debates   10

2   Collaborative Building and Tinkering: Toward a
DH-Inflected Approach to L2 Learning and Teaching   22

3   Implementing a DHL2 Classroom: Design, Learner
Characteristics, and Assessment   35

4   DH Tools and Examples: A Case Study through
Cultural Comparison   47

Conclusion: Challenges and Considerations of a DHL2
Methodology   63

Appendix: List of Digital Resources 67

Bibliography 69

About the Author 77

Acknowledgments

I am grateful to a number of people for their generous support of this project. The impetus for this project came from a discussion with Clara Totten, Languages Acquisitions Editor at Georgetown University Press, who contacted me regarding a presentation I gave at the American Association of Teachers of French in 2017 on a collaborative course I had designed with my colleague, Kathleen Antonioli, on teaching translation and the challenges of implementing a DH project in the L2 classroom. I am grateful to Clara for her encouragement, advice, and support throughout the writing process. I would also like to thank Lauren Coats, Emily McGinn, and the Office of Digital Humanities at the National Endowment for the Humanities for generously supporting my participation in the "Textual Data & Digital Texts in the Undergraduate Classroom" 2018–2019 institute. Their workshop gave me a place to learn, test, and tinker freely and collaboratively in the very best tradition of DH practices. My thanks go also to my colleagues and students in the Department of Modern Languages at Kansas State University who have either tinkered along with me or tested these ideas bravely, including Kathleen Antonioli, Sara Kearns, and students in FREN 720 in fall 2016, FREN 711 in spring 2018, and FREN 713 in fall 2018. I would also like to thank Necia Chronister for her perceptive comments and advice on the revision of chapter 1. Finally, but certainly not least, my warmest thanks to my sister, Rebecca, for her invaluable advice from the perspective of a high school English teacher and her wonderful wit; to my parents, for their unfailing support at all times, and to my husband, Ryan, not only for his unending patience and technical know-how but for his steadfast love that makes all things worthwhile.

Abbreviations

ACTFL	American Council on the Teaching of Foreign Languages
API	Google Maps Application Programming Interface
DH	digital humanities
DHL2	digital humanities–inflected second language
DHML	modern language and digital humanities framework
DHQ	*Digital Humanities Quarterly*
DiRT	digital research tools
GIS	geographic information systems
HASTAC	Humanities, Arts, Science, and Technology Alliance and Collaboratory
L1	first language
L2	second language
ML	modern language
MLA	Modern Language Association
NNS	non-native speaker
NS	native speaker
SLA	second language acquisition
ZPD	zone of proximal development

Introduction

How Does the Second Language Classroom Benefit from the Digital Humanities?

WHAT IS/ARE THE digital humanities (DH), and what does it / do they have to do with language learning? The grammatical uncertainty surrounding the title of the discipline alone should signal the plurality and perennial shift associated with it.[1] I first stumbled upon the digital humanities a few years ago, unaware of the full scope of the discipline, let alone its potential for second language pedagogy. However, as I implemented various projects in my own French language courses, I began to understand the true implications and possibilities of a digital humanities–inflected program—that is, a meaningful approach to language learning that is content-driven and task-based, collaborative, and communicative. In this book, I propose a methodological and theoretical approach to language pedagogy informed by the digital humanities.

It is imperative that humanists as a whole, and modern languages specialists in particular, become more familiar with the digital humanities. As William Pannapacker (2011) has noted, "The digital humanities are not some flashy new theory that might go out of fashion. At this point, the digital humanities are The Thing. There's no Next about it. And it won't be long until the digital humanities are, quite simply, 'the humanities.'" This book, designed with the nonspecialist in mind, aims at once to provide an overview of the theoretical basis of the digital humanities while simultaneously introducing the reader to its applications in the second language classroom. The digital humanities offer a methodological approach that, if applied, could both enhance and facilitate the pedagogical approaches already at play in many second language classrooms.

The approaches encompassed by DH are varied and diverse. They range from projects like **Danteworlds**,* a multimedia, interaction-rich resource on the *Divine Comedy* directed by Guy P. Raffa at the University of Texas at Austin (Raffa n.d.), to the **Quantitative Formalism** project at Stanford, which seeks to explore whether "computer-generated algorithms could 'recognize' literary genres," specifically whether a text is an example of a gothic novel or a bildungsroman (Allison et al. 2011). A DH project may use mapping technology (Geographic Information System applications, GIS) to plot locations in a novel, like the **Mapping the Astrée** project at Kansas State University (Cro and O'Dea n.d.), or to map the emotions of a city, as exemplified in the **Emotions of London** project in the Stanford Literary Lab (Heuser, Moretti, and Steiner 2016). The projects undertaken are as diverse as their practitioners and depend primarily on the type of questions one seeks to answer and whether those questions might be served by the application of computational methods.

Given the rising interest in the globalization of DH, the ways in which DH is practiced in non-anglophone environments, and questions raised like those by Pitman and Taylor (2017) in their article "Where's the ML [Modern Languages] in DH? And Where's the DH in ML?" a consideration of the application of digital humanities in the modern languages classroom is a much-needed intervention in the field. As the recent special issue of *Digital Humanities Quarterly* (*DHQ*) attests (12.1, 2018), DH is a global discipline that is practiced not only in geographically diverse locations but across multiple languages, each with its own culturally conditioned expectations regarding research, the humanities, and the place of the digital in said enterprise. Nonetheless, many of the theories about DH have been formulated in either US or British academic circles, resulting in a perception that DH belongs primarily in English or history departments. The linguistic and geographic specificities of varying global DH practices challenge the perceived anglophone hegemony of the field while also evoking the need for plurilingual and pluricultural awareness among practitioners. Take, for example, the creation in 2014 of Humanistica, the first international association devoted to digital humanities within a particular linguistic and cultural context (Francophone). Humanistica seeks to assemble

---

* Bolded terms appear in an appendix of digital resources located at the back of the book.

and connect all French-language researchers using digital humanities in their projects as well as to support specific DH projects themselves, a potent reminder of the plurilingual and multicultural reality of DH today.

To bring to light the global nature of DH, Pitman and Taylor (2017) call for a "Modern Languages–inflected Digital Humanities." They describe such a practice as a reflective, analytical awareness of the pluricultural and plurilingual reality of digital culture, despite the anglophone-dominated digital cultural theory that accompanies and tempers the field. They see the digital humanities and modern languages as trans- or interdisciplinary fields that share a great deal of scope (for example, both attract practitioners from a variety of humanities disciplines, including literature, history, philosophy, art, and cultural studies) and call for a "hybrid Modern Languages and Digital Humanities framework" that they term a "critical DHML" (2017, para. 33), affirming that a critical approach to the digital humanities enhanced by modern languages would allow its practitioners to "explore how cultural identities that transgress nation-state boundaries may be expressed and enabled through digital technologies, how non-Anglophone or plurilingual contexts might provide us with models for understanding the processes of de- and re-territorialisation offered by many digital technologies" (2017, para. 31).

For practical purposes, this guide seeks to explore the inverse of what Pitman and Taylor propose: a DH-inflected modern languages classroom. While there has been an ideological shift recently to examine the nature of "global DH" within a plurilingual reality, such an approach has not yet conditioned the extant pedagogical literature. Indeed, DH centers are most commonly found in English departments or in specialized centers within the academic library. Additionally, pedagogy has formed an increasingly important area of inquiry in DH in recent years, especially in terms of inflecting non-DH courses with DH methods and tools. In 2015, Eileen Gardner and Ronald G. Musto published *The Digital Humanities: A Primer for Students and Scholars*, which provides a detailed overview of the humanities, the place of the digital therein, lists of DH tools, and a robust theoretical examination of the potential and challenges DH represents. Yet the volume does not specifically address the challenges of inflecting the second language (L2) classroom with DH methodology, despite drawing from a linguistically diverse set of projects as illustrative of the scope of the field. More recently, a special issue of *DHQ* (11.3, 2017) was devoted to the digital humanities in the undergraduate classroom, again providing rich avenues for exploring the pedagogical ramifications for DH but without a focus on modern language courses and the ensuing pedagogical implications. The same year, Battershill and Ross (2017) published an introductory guide to DH pedagogy, *Using Digital Humanities in the Classroom: A Practical Introduction for Teachers, Lecturers, and Students*. While this guide offers a variety of suggestions, possible rubrics, assignment ideas, and tools, it does so again without a consideration of language. That is, the authors tend to assume the reader is either working in an anglophone environment or is teaching either in English or through the digital humanities. The challenge, then, is how to effectively transfer a DH pedagogy into the L2 curriculum.

I would argue that what has excited many humanists as they explore the digital humanities is the intentionality and engagement inherent in its methodology. Design and building are the primary foci of DH, from thinking carefully about the research process to considering how to communicate the discovery to the public. Reassuring for practitioners is the knowledge that the field welcomes innovative and collaborative approaches perceived as nontraditional. These are not new characteristics to the humanities. Rather, their reformulation and movement to the forefront tend to demystify humanistic analysis and research, opening it up as a shared practice inscribed in social and cultural terms. It is often described as a highly democratic method of engagement that destabilizes traditional notions of authority and leads toward a more open and cooperative model for scholarship and teaching. I would argue that in this respect Pitman and Taylor (2017) are quite right when they affirm that modern languages and the digital humanities have a great deal in common.

Language learning is a social, cultural, and cooperative practice that engages the same type of methodology and procedure as is endemic to DH. In the L2 classroom, the instructor often serves as facilitator rather than singular authority. Group work and one-on-one dialogue, situated in project- and task-based learning, are characteristic of best practices of L2 instruction, and collaboration is essential to a truly communicative enterprise. Language is a reciprocal, active, and engaging practice that takes place in a speech community and is therefore highly social. The importance of collaboration in both DH and L2 acquisition forms a productive intersection between the two fields, particularly in terms of our understanding of the learner:

> In a sociocultural view of SLA [second language acquisition] the learner is not just an individual who on encountering a foreign language processes

and assimilates vocabulary and syntax. Rather, learners are seen to participate in different speech communities where they draw on social resources
(other participants, institutional affordances), material resources (PCs, networks, applications), and semiotic resources (signs, genres). (Lund 2008, 39)

This is a propitious time to be examining what DH can bring to the L2
classroom, and the examination is long overdue given the potential for
enhancing what is already happening there.

To DH or Not to DH? The Answer Is Yes!

On whether to include DH methods into non-DH classrooms, Kara
Kennedy's response is emphatically yes:

It is an ethical duty and a feminist imperative. Humanities students need
digital literacy skills—including the women who make up the majority of
such students and potentially face gender biases related to digital technology and computing culture—and DH tools and methods are well-oriented
toward the development of these skills within the context of the humanities.
(Kennedy 2017)

Kennedy here underscores the practicality and professionalization inherent within a DH approach. These benefits are often identified as a core
argument for incorporating the digital into humanities courses (Davidson
2008; Davis 2013; Harris 2013; Clò 2016; Battershill and Ross 2017; Locke
2017). Such a perspective recognizes the potential that DH offers humanities courses often characterized as "impractical" by critics. That it echoes
the practicality already represented by modern language courses further
bolsters the argument for a critical DHML, or, perhaps more accurately
when considering methodology and acquisition, a DH-inflected second
language (DHL2) pedagogy.

However, the argument to incorporate DH into the language classroom,
to fold the practices and methodologies of the discipline into L2 courses,
extends beyond the practical in terms of a response to political and institutional pressures. Kennedy points to inclusivity and gender equality as
benefits of a DH-inflected training. Additionally, it corresponds to a
deeper societal need for informational and digital literacy. Seen as exten-
sions of digital readiness, or an individual's preparedness to use tech tools
to pursue learning, digital literacy is an important metric in today's

technology-oriented world yet remains underrepresented in pedagogy. A recent Pew report indicates that there are still significant gaps in digital readiness among US adults (Horrigan 2016). Over half of US adults score on the lower end of the digital preparedness spectrum, characterized as either unprepared or unwilling to use tech tools, a lack of confidence in the ability to use tech tools in various contexts (particularly educational), and misgivings over evaluating truthfulness and accuracy in information conveyed through digital resources. This alarming reality reaches the core of the imperative to increase digital literacy among students to facilitate their transition into the post-scholastic world.

Coupled with the need to increase digital literacy is the need to offer access to opportunities that may not be present in the student's life outside the classroom. Barriers to accessibility exist, and the previously identified "digital divide" between "digital natives" and "digital immigrants"[2] focusing on generational divide in digital familiarity (Prensky 2001) ignores the roles that race, gender, economics, and geography play in an individual's level of digital readiness (Locke 2017). Nonetheless, instructors tend to conceive of students as digital natives without regard for or awareness of the learners' actual experience with the digital (Bennett and Maton 2011; Locke 2017). A DH-inflected classroom, with an emphasis on scaffolded and structured interactions with technology, may at once address the gaps in digital readiness while affording opportunities to ensure that all students are equally prepared for entry into the workforce. The critical engagement and distance fostered in the L2 classroom encourage procedural approaches to activities and objects that will complement and support movement toward digital literacy.

Organization

This guide is divided into short chapters that seek to introduce current practitioners as well as practitioners-in-training to the basic DH methodological approaches and tools of interest for second language instruction in both higher and secondary educational contexts. Inevitably, given the rapid developments and progress inherent in the digital field, this volume will not be comprehensive; the field expands daily as designers create new tools and consider new ways to use existing ones. This guide does not propose to be exhaustive, but rather to serve as a starting point—a description of the field and the predominant methodological approaches that condition work in the digital humanities. This methodology dictates a certain pedagogy that may be fruitfully applied in the second language classroom.

The first chapter ("The Digital Humanities: Definitions and Debates") offers an introduction to the discipline and identifies core tenets that will form our primary point of focus as we explore a DHL2 pedagogy. The digital humanities, albeit already in possession of a significant history—in the earlier form of humanities computing and most recently in its "digital humanities" classification—remains a field in flux. Its practitioners are divided across the spectrum of users, ranging from "big tenters" who believe in inclusive definitions and modes of practice to those who construe the field's parameters more narrowly, defining practitioners as those who code and design tools specifically for each project undertaken. The author of this study belongs to the former camp, that which defines the digital humanities openly and inclusively to permit various manifestations of the same. This opens the field to encompass those who utilize the rich tools already at our disposal, either through the work of other digital humanists or through public or private technological endeavors. This chapter will offer an overview of the various definitions of the digital humanities and the contribution of each to the understanding of a larger methodological approach, which conditions how we teach DH, particularly in the second language classroom (a context often under-examined if not outright ignored).[3]

The second chapter ("Collaborative Building and Tinkering: Toward a DH-Inflected Approach to L2 Learning and Teaching") will provide an overview of points of contact between L2 and DH pedagogy that will help to inform the implementation of DH methodology in the L2 classroom. Integral to this section will be a consideration of how DH can enrich the second language classroom by highlighting best practices in the field, particularly in terms of communicative, task-based, and content-based approaches to language instruction. I propose paralleling digital and linguistic proficiency as a conceptual model to facilitate framing learning objectives and course design. Additionally, I suggest varying levels of engagement for measuring degrees of DH inflection, allowing instructors to consider to what degree they want to engage with the digital in the L2 classroom.

An examination of course and assignment design and evaluation will be the focus of the third chapter ("Implementing a DHL2 Classroom: Design, Learner Characteristics, and Assessment"). How does one design student-centered assignments and courses in a highly collaborative, L2-focused environment concentrated on project development wherein success may not ultimately be defined in facile terms of "completion"? The nature of digital humanities work frequently defies the timeline and schedule of the traditional classroom as these projects and the data collection for them necessitate a complex process involving design and analysis that may exceed the scope of the traditional term project. A digital humanities–inflected curriculum requires patience, innovation, flexibility, and a penchant for problem solving, particularly when confronted by the unexpected. This section also addresses some of the challenges engendered by a digital humanities approach. There is inevitable anxiety concerning ownership of intellectual property in predominantly open-access, online environments. Moreover, students at times bristle at the thought of group work, so examining the possible means of motivating and scaffolding DH collaboration will be essential to the success of such an approach.

The fourth chapter ("DH Tools and Examples: A Case Study through Cultural Comparison") capitalizes on a case study approach to illustrate the possible breadth and richness of a DH methodology while describing types of approaches, activities, and tools that may be used to complete a particular type of task. Practical examples, such as specific tools and activities as well as descriptions of how to scaffold tasks for various levels of linguistic and digital proficiency, will form the core of this section to illustrate the methodology.

The text closes with a brief conclusion that seeks to offer a consideration of some challenges that a DHL2 pedagogy represents, particularly in terms of resource allocation and support. The instructor's institution and the financial resources available therein will determine the degree to which one may feel comfortable inflecting one's courses. Fortunately, there are a number of freely available tools that make implementing a DHL2 approach very feasible. Another consideration is that there is a real investment needed in terms of time, particularly when first experimenting with a DHL2. It is the hope of the author that this guide makes clear why such an investment is worthwhile.

A brief word on the structure of each chapter—an overview of the subject will introduce each chapter, while at the end the reader will find a summary and reflection questions and activities to stimulate discussion and to facilitate adoption of this guide in a pedagogical context. In addition, key reference works will be recommended for further reading on related topics after each chapter. At the end of the volume, the reader will find a comprehensive list of references consulted by the author in the preparation of this work, which may be of use to the reader interested in exploring the field in greater detail.

Notes

1. Indeed, practitioners alternately use the singular or the plural, although the singular seems to be increasing in number (about double the number of Google results return for "Digital Humanities is" over "are").

2. A "digital native" is one who grew up in the digital era with easy access to technology (i.e., computers, smartphones, social media platforms, etc.) whereas a "digital immigrant" is one who grew up in an analog world and learned how to use digital technology. While there is a general perception that those students who are digital natives would have an inherent understanding of how to use technology, the reality is that they are often just as lost if not more so than the digital immigrant and require explicit instruction on digital tools in a pedagogical setting.

3. As mentioned above, it should be noted that this status quo is changing. The most recent issue of *Digital Humanities Quarterly* (12.1, 2018) featured two special rubrics: the first, a Spanish-language special issue, and the second, a French-language special issue. Contributions were written in either Spanish or French, and an English-language translation of the abstract was offered. According to the authors of the introduction to the French-language section, the purpose was "to draw the attention of regular readers of the journal to work from the francophone world, and to better connect francophone networks with international communities in the field" in recognition of the increasing globalization of the field (Berra et al. 2018).

1

The Digital Humanities: Definitions and Debates

THE HUMANITIES HAVE undergone a shift recently, wherein scholars seek to take advantage of the advent of new and increasingly accessible forms of technology to facilitate the collection and analysis of big data. Tom Scheinfeldt has likened these new technological approaches in the humanities in which information is evaluated in new and unanticipated ways to the desire of late nineteenth- and early twentieth-century scholars to catalog the expanding range of information made available through advents in technology and science (P. Cohen 2010). Other scholars see the move from print to digital as analogous to the "flowering of Renaissance and post-Renaissance print culture" (Burdick et al. 2012). Notwithstanding the numerous articles and entries proposing to define the digital humanities, a clear and concise definition remains elusive, in part due to conflation regarding the purpose and nature of the practice itself. This chapter proposes an understanding of the digital humanities as a transdisciplinary or interdisciplinary endeavor characterized by a specific methodology that is particularly well suited for adaptation and use in the second language classroom.

Background

The digital humanities, as a practice of humanistic endeavor, is far older than one might assume given the current hype surrounding the field. The origins of what is today classified as the digital humanities may be traced to an early computing project undertaken by an Italian Jesuit priest, Roberto Busa, who, in 1949, embarked on an effort to create a concordance of St. Thomas Aquinas and related authors' works. The total was around 11 million words of medieval Latin. Busa hypothesized that a machine might facilitate the process and reached out to IBM for support. The texts were transferred to punch cards and then a concordance program was written to sort and organize the words under their dictionary headings (a fuller, more detailed account is given in Hockey 2004). This is the earliest example of computers being utilized for humanistic purposes.

Originally called "humanities computing," the discipline was born from the desire to capitalize on advances in computer sciences to facilitate complex statistical and computational tasks in textual analysis (for example, lexical analyses in various texts inputted into the system). While disparate projects utilizing machines and computing in the humanities may be documented in the 50s and 60s (the journal *Computers and the Humanities* was founded in 1966), it was not until the subsequent decades (from the 70s to the mid-80s) that the field began to consolidate, as Susan Hockey (2004) puts it. At this time, numerous associations rose up (for example, The Association for Literary and Linguistic Computing, International Conference on Computing in the Humanities, and most recently the Alliance of Digital Humanities Organizations, which welcomes under its umbrella six different international organizations, including the Association for Computers and the Humanities). Such organizations provided more regular opportunities for communication and interaction between digital humanists and ultimately led to greater institutionalized support for its practitioners. In the 80s, questions were raised over whether students should be taught humanities computing, but challenges such as accessibility, affordability, and need for institutional support (both in terms of infrastructure and funding), coupled with the challenges of memory storage, made humanities computing prohibitively costly.

With the dawn of the internet in the 1990s, the potential for the digital humanities and its possibility of widespread dissemination became more tangible, lending a greater urgency to developing standards of practice while simultaneously training humanists to participate in the rapidly expanding field. Not coincidentally, the increase in memory available on modern computers also helped to shift and expand the scope of the digital humanities. While research universities have begun in the last fifteen to twenty years to launch digital humanities centers in partnership with their libraries and various departments, federal agencies like the National

Endowment for the Humanities recognized the potential that digital humanities represented for facilitating its own mission of "making the humanities available to all Americans" ("Strategic Plan" 2018), launching the Office of Digital Humanities in 2008.

Today, the digital humanities is far more than a collection of markup languages, text encoding practices, and computational tools to be accessed by faculty and instructors interested in harnessing technology in the classroom. Rather, DH is most effective when used as a methodological approach to the discipline under study, such as content-based courses in a target language. Such an approach necessitates, however, a slight shift in perspective. The content studied (for example, a literary survey or cultural course) may be explored through freely accessible DH tools that permit visualization and analysis of the texts in ways that offer multiple means of approaching them. The union of "big data" methods (i.e., statistical analysis, distant reading) with close reading and visualization, helps students to explore the textual from a new perspective that enriches the possible learning outcomes. However, DH extends beyond the textual realm. For example, Gardiner and Musto (2015) outline "elements" that they propose are constitutive of humanistic study: text, document, object, artifact, image, video, sound, and space. This chapter will explore a few definitions of DH that are particularly useful in framing a DH-inflected pedagogy in the L2 classroom.

Definitions

Defining the digital humanities has occupied a particularly large swath of the literature in the field, so much so that it has almost become a genre unto itself. The fascination with ontological questions has been, in part, a response to various pressures from disparate segments of the profession, ranging from dubious peers in the humanities suspicious of the use of digital methods in traditionally material- and text-based disciplines to college administrators intrigued by the potential to attract interested students but reticent to invest funds in new endeavors. Perhaps most challenging of all has been the preference in the academy and in various institutions of higher education for traditional, recognizable forms of scholarship (i.e., article, monograph), particularly when it comes to questions of promotion and tenure (Burdick et al. 2012; Gardiner and Musto 2015). Hence the urgency to define and problematize the work being done in the digital humanities and the primacy of discussions related to research and publication. Numerous manifestos have been published exploring definitions of the discipline, both in traditional print form (such as the anthology, *Defining the Digital Humanities: A Reader* assembled by Terras, Nyhan, and Vanhoutte 2013) and online through openly accessible journals, like *Digital Humanities Quarterly* (*DHQ*). Indeed, in the face of the call to participate publicly and openly in the question, there are an increasing number of practitioners' own blogs and websites wherein individuals contribute their own definitions of the discipline and how it informs practices in their own research; consider, for example, either Ted Underwood's (Underwood n.d.) or Katherine D. Harris's blog (Harris n.d.). The *Chronicle of Higher Education* has featured several articles on the digital humanities, examining the multiple sides of the discipline, including critiques that question the validity and import of the field and responses to the same (Brennan 2017; Long, Bond, and Underwood 2017; Weiskott 2017). All this activity has helped to tease out the finer points of the discipline.

While I do not propose to rehash all the various perspectives on the question of purpose and function in DH, there are certain shared characteristics among definitions of the field that are particularly relevant for L2 instructors and for establishing the methodology inherent in DH. First and foremost, DH is about making or building. As Stephen Ramsay (Ramsay 2013b) notoriously affirmed in a talk at the MLA that sparked a great deal of controversy in the community,

> Personally, I think Digital Humanities is about building things. I'm willing to entertain highly expansive definitions of what it means to build something. I also think the discipline includes and should include people who theorize about building, people who design so that others might build, and those who supervise building. . . . But if you are not making anything, you are not . . . a digital humanist. (241)

Put another way, it is an applied practice that focuses on projects and production or fabrication, tempting comparisons with artisanal culture:

> We should be able to be clear about the importance of project management and thing knowledge—the tacit knowledge of fabrication and its cultures— even if the very nature of that *poesis* (knowledge of making) itself cannot easily (and shouldn't have to) be put into words. . . . We should be able to explain that there is real knowledge in the making and that that knowledge can be acquired by anyone genuinely interested. (Rockwell 2013)

Continuing along these lines, the authors of *Digital_Humanities* affirm the purpose of DH in similar terms:

> Digital Humanities represents a major expansion of the purview of the humanities, precisely because it brings the values, representation and interpretive practices, meaning-making strategies, complexities, and ambiguities of being human into every realm of experience and knowledge of the world. It is a global, trans-historical and transmedia approach to knowledge and meaning-making. (Burdick et al. 2012, vii)

Burdick et al. continue by describing DH as "conspicuously collaborative and generative," which challenges the traditional model of humanities research (consisting mainly of single-authored monographs), opting for cooperative endeavors that necessitate plurality in design and execution (3). What comes through clearly is the importance of intentionality and the emphasis on conscientious and open engagement with materials and questions of research design.

While some have underscored building in conceptions of DH (Ramsay 2013a, 2013b), Mark Sample (2011) has focused on sharing:

> The heart of the digital humanities is not the production of knowledge; it's the reproduction of knowledge. . . . The promise of the digital is not in the way it allows us to ask new questions because of digital tools or because of new methodologies made possible by those tools. The promise is in the way the digital reshapes the representation, sharing, and discussion of knowledge. We are no longer bound by the physical demands of printed books and paper journals, no longer constrained by production costs and distribution friction, no longer hampered by a top-down and unsustainable business model. And we should no longer be content to make our work public achingly slowly along ingrained routes, authors and readers alike delayed by innumerable gateways limiting knowledge production and sharing.

The focus on design and the open nature of many DH projects leads naturally to considerations of accessibility and the potential for immediate, public engagement. Matthew Kirschenbaum (2010) underscores the social nature of DH that lends not only to the cooperative character of the discipline but to the visibility of the same in public spheres beyond traditional, academic outlets (i.e., specialized research journals obtainable only through institutional access). DH-ers utilize social media in concrete and effective ways, and the projects that DH-ers design are often freely accessible to the public. Sample's observations regarding the immediacy and interactivity that DH offers do not negate the importance that Ramsay and others have identified in building; in essence, they are two complementary sides to the same coin.

One question that is central to the debate is that of inclusion or exclusion. In attempting to define the field, several have also attempted to limit it in an effort to delineate what its practitioners do as distinct from conceptions of the humanities as a whole. This tendency toward limitation has led to a schism between more inclusive stances (such as those taken on by "big tenters" who see DH as open to an array of possible configurations) and those that are more exclusive, offering specialized descriptions and alluding to specific skillsets that render the field less accessible to the non-specialist. In an all-inclusive view of the field, there is concern that it may be too all-encompassing. This position reflects Melissa Terras's concern that big tent ideology reduces that which distinguishes DH from other forms of scholarly pursuit (Terras 2013). Burdick et al. (2012) propose, in their "Short Guide to the Digital_Humanities" (the final pages of their larger monograph on the subject, *Digital_Humanities*), to define both what is and what is not digital humanities, echoing as they do so John Unsworth's consideration (2002) of what does (and does not) constitute humanities computing. In Burdick et al.'s definition, they challenge the primacy of text and print in humanistic inquiry:

> Digital Humanities marks a move beyond a privileging of the textual, emphasizing graphical methods of knowledge production and organization, design as an integral component of research, transmedia crisscrossings, and an expanded concept of the sensorium of humanistic knowledge. It is also characterized by an intensified focus on the building of transferrable tools, environments, and platforms for collaborative scholarly work and by an emphasis upon curation as a defining feature of scholarly practice. (2012, 122)

Some have read in Burdick et al. and others a tendency toward exclusion, particularly when they affirm, "The mere use of digital tools for the purpose of humanistic research and communication does not qualify as Digital Humanities" (2012, 122). That is, without coding or programming skills, or graphic design capabilities, one may not actually fully participate in DH.

Perhaps one of the most cohesive and convincing rebuttals of this exclusive stance is Katherine Harris's cogent arguments that underscore the institutional realities in which many DH practitioners find themselves. Harris (2013) asks why the use of digital tools for humanistic research is *not* part of DH. She explains that the way in which her institution is set up does not lend itself to DH as conceived by Burdick et al. The emphasis on coding, programming, and design over use of digital tools excludes a large swath of practitioners from the field. Rather, in her view, her students gain insight through serving as "the advisory board or the editorial board of a project" (2013, 22). She asserts,

> Teaching at a non-R1 and doing Digital Humanities requires a certain do-it-yourself (DIY) ethos. But, DIY also implies uncompensated and often-times un-credited work. For the longest time Digital Humanities has advocated going out and doing. Being plucky. Taking the initiative. At a non-R1, this means teaching classes, writing traditional scholarship, then, and only then, adding some Digital Humanities sauce to everything else. There just isn't time. The only way to combat that encroaching workload is to engage students in Digital Humanities—basically to throw them in the deep end of Digital Humanities with some guidance to see how they break it. And break it they do. (2013, 21)

For Harris, one of the core benefits and characteristics of DH is that it shifts thinking away from linear textuality and embraces process over product. She contends that DH-based approaches permit and encourage empowerment and that her students engage in active and creative ways with technology, a much-needed activity in today's ever-increasingly technical global landscape. Conversely, Ted Underwood admits that he entered the field assuming that he would be able to use the publicly available extant toolsets for text mining, like Voyant, before realizing that they did not necessarily correspond to his needs, and before long he was learning to program to facilitate his research plans (Underwood 2012). However, this is perhaps the distinction between teaching and research as well as the acknowledgment of varying levels of engagement in DH. One may absolutely utilize the tools readily available, and I will propose this as the primary means for pedagogical engagement in DHL2 (a shift from Pitman and Taylor's conception of DHML to focus on the pedagogical aspect of second language learning and acquisition). Nonetheless, there may come a time in a researcher's agenda when designing and building takes on a different meaning, and it would be disingenuous to suppose that programming would never come into play. While Battershill and Ross (2017) affirm optimistically that the debate regarding coding as a central aspect to DH is over, that seems an exaggerated claim; after all, the issue was presented as central in Terras, Nyhan, and Vanhoutte's reader (2013) and continues to be examined in various venues, including blog posts on HASTAC (Humanities, Arts, Science, and Technology Alliance and Collaboratory). Perhaps the tenor of the discussion has changed, however; rather than seeing coding as a means for exclusion, programming, or at least a basic awareness of how programming functions, is presented as an opportunity to enhance and facilitate research in a useful and accessible way in recent HASTAC blogs (Hunter 2016; Pottroff 2015; Faith 2013).

Core Characteristics of Digital Pedagogy

Ultimately, there is no single definition of the digital humanities that may incorporate all the varied characteristics of the field. However, one may identify certain values that are shared by DH practitioners. Lisa Spiro (2012) identifies the core values of the digital humanities as openness (in terms of the exchange of ideas, the development of content, and the transparency of the field), collaboration (much of the work done in DH is cooperative in nature), collegiality and connectedness (describing the inclusiveness of the field, notwithstanding recent debates between what William Pannapacker [2011] has termed the "builders and theorizers, coders and non-coders"), diversity (of professionals, class, race, gender, etc.), and experimentation (the experimental nature of the digital humanities has given rise to DH centers that follow the laboratory model—i.e., the University of Virginia's Scholars Lab and the Stanford Literary Lab). These are the same values that Davis et al. (2016) identify in their introduction to the Modern Language Association (MLA) Commons site of fifty carefully curated keywords and accompanying pedagogical artifacts that they identify as evocative and central to conceptions of digital pedagogy.

In contrast, or perhaps more specifically, Harris identifies "mainstays" that characterize work in the digital humanities and that she sees as central to digital pedagogy: collaboration, process, building, and tinkering, all captured under the heading of "screwing around" (2013, 7), a nod to the digital practices that are often contrasted with their "serious" and "traditional" humanities counterparts, borrowed from Stephen Ramsay's 2010 talk.[1] These values do, indeed, provide a road map, as it were, for work in the digital humanities, so much so that I offer the following definition of the field for the purposes of this book: the digital humanities is a productive practice conditioned by open, inclusive, and collaborative project work that is reflectively designed around humanistic inquiry and often culminates in openly accessible (i.e., public) artifacts in the digital realm. This is the definition we will use as our starting point for examining, in the following section, how to implement said approach in the L2 classroom.

Digital Pedagogy and Technology in Language Learning

A final aspect of digital humanities to consider, in relation to definitions and pedagogy in particular, is that of digital pedagogy. The term has become more widely accepted of late and is used by various practitioners (Harris 2013; Davis et al. 2016; Kennedy 2017) to describe a use of digital technology in pedagogical contexts that is reflective in nature. While it is tempting to make comparisons and parallels with proponents of technology in the L2 classroom, it is important to note that a pedagogy inflected with digital humanities methodology is distinct from examinations that focus on technology in the L2 classroom such as Marta González-Lloret's text, *A Practical Guide to Integrating Technology into Task-Based Language Teaching* (González-Lloret 2016), Robert J. Blake's *Brave New Digital Classroom: Technology and Foreign Language Learning* (2008), or studies on the role of digital games on L2 learning and teaching (Sykes 2011, 2018; Holden and Sykes 2011; Reinhardt and Sykes 2014). As Katherine Harris puts it succinctly, "Digital Pedagogy is not about the tools" (Harris 2013, 19). For proponents of technology in the L2 classroom, it is imperative for the instructor to consider the ramifications of technological choices in relation to learning objectives and to scaffold technological interactions accordingly. However, digital pedagogy explicitly involves the students in the process of reflection, selection, design, and evaluation. This represents a distinct difference between the two approaches, revolving around questions of intentionality and design.

While technology will form a natural nexus of investigation, DH-inflected approaches should not be conflated with those describing the use of technology in the classroom, such as computer assisted language learning. DH represents a reflexive practice deeply embedded in humanistic inquiry. DHL2 methodology, while promoting language acquisition, describes more accurately a mode of instruction that capitalizes on the digital advances to facilitate collaborative and cooperative modes of learning while considering reflectively the act of building and making in a digital frame. In short, while DH pedagogy involves technology, not all technology-driven practices of instruction involve DH.

Predominantly project-based, DHL2 stems from content-based language instructional approaches and is centered on designing research questions and working collaboratively to pursue answers. The results of such projects may be delivered in a public forum of some sort, capitalizing on digital tools and increasing the immediacy and reach of humanities research and instruction. Such an approach is evocative of task-based methodologies for language instruction, with one caveat—while task-based approaches often incite students to imitate or mimic real-world tasks and interactions, a DH-inflected program is built around actual, real-world tasks that will ultimately be folded into the fabric of the target-language material and digital cultural reality. Students in DH-inflected courses participate in ongoing dialogues on issues of importance as related to the course content and frequently, in the context of higher education, intrinsically linked to the instructor's area of expertise and research. The end result is far more immediate and, dare I say, relevant because it impacts the fabric of the world and cultures studied.

Such a position corresponds nicely to the firm belief inherent within DH pedagogy that all DH work is about making and building (Burdick et al. 2012; Ramsay 2013a) and that the results should, ultimately, be shareable with a larger public that extends beyond the confines of the classroom (Sample 2011). The students in a DH-inflected course delve into the L2 digital world immediately, gaining opportunities to use their language skills in a range of tasks with both the closed community of the class and the larger L2 community. Throughout, our focus will be on practical strategies for harnessing the unique approach to research and learning offered by the digital humanities to enhance instruction and learning strategies in the second language classroom. Characterized by active engagement, preparation of deliverables, and new models for exploring content, this approach capitalizes on task-based and content-based methods for language instruction. The implementation of DH strategies in the L2 classroom contributes to the generation of a meaningful bridge between classroom experience and professional endeavors for students across L2 curricula.

Summary

In this chapter, we examined a variety of definitions for the digital humanities (DH). Certain shared characteristics across varying perspectives are as follows: DH involves using digital and computational methods and tools in varying modes of humanistic inquiry. Such a practice involves building and design, both of research questions and of projects. It is a deeply collaborative approach that belies images of the lone scholar producing knowledge in limited and inaccessible ways. The nature of the digital permits sharing knowledge production in an unprecedented way, lending a public nature and increased awareness to pursuits in DH. The discipline privileges a focus on design and building that is openly accessible. Such a focus in terms of work product results in a pedagogy that values experimentation, collaboration, creation, and process in learning. In the following section we will explore in greater detail how to inflect the L2 classroom with a DH approach.

Reflection Questions and Activities

1. Do you have any experience with the digital humanities? Have you ever participated in a DH project? If so, what was it like? If not, are you aware of any DH projects? Do a quick internet search and record the results that you find.
2. After reading this chapter and considering your personal experiences as well as the internet search you conducted, offer your own working definition of the digital humanities.
3. Discuss the difference between the inclusive and exclusionary views of DH. On what side of the fence do you find yourself? Why?
4. How might a DH-inflected course design differ from incorporating technology in the L2 classroom? Explain.

Recommended Further Reading

Burdick, Anne, Johanna Drucker, Peter Lunenfeld, Todd Presner, and Jeffrey Schnapp. 2012. *Digital_Humanities*. Cambridge, MA: MIT Press.

Davis, Rebecca Frost, Matthew K. Gold, Katherine D. Harris, and Jentery Sayers, eds. 2016. *Digital Pedagogy in the Humanities: Concepts, Models, and Experiments*. MLA Commons. https://digitalpedagogy.mla.hcommons.org/.

Gardiner, Eileen, and Ronald G. Musto. 2015. *The Digital Humanities: A Primer for Students and Scholars*. New York: Cambridge University Press.

Hirsch, Brett D., ed. 2012. *Digital Humanities Pedagogy: Practices, Principles and Politics*. Open Book Publishers. https://doi.org/10.11647/OBP.0024.

Terras, Melissa, Julianne Nyhan, and Edward Vanhoutte, eds. 2013. *Defining Digital Humanities: A Reader*. London: Routledge. https://www.routledge.com /Defining-Digital-Humanities-A-Reader/Terras-Nyhan-Vanhoutte/p/book /9781409469636.

Note

1. This talk is now available in a published collection, *Pastplay: Teaching and Learning History with Technology* (2014). Citations come from this edition.

2

Collaborative Building and Tinkering: Toward a DH-Inflected Approach to L2 Learning and Teaching

THIS CHAPTER DESCRIBES the pedagogical basis for a DH-inflected approach to second language learning and teaching by highlighting points of similarity and contact between the methodological approaches to the two fields. In SLA, communicative approaches may be characterized as weak, medium, or strong, depending on the level of immersion and the centrality of meaningful communication to the pedagogical design. Similarly, courses may be inflected with one of three possible levels of DH inflection: strong, medium, or weak. The level of DH inflection is tied to the degree of integration of DH into the L2 in the class, ranging from a single-day activity (a weak inflection) to a multiday project (a medium inflection) to an entire course (a strong inflection). A course utilizing DHL2 throughout may be qualified as a "strong" communicative approach that is highly immersive in both linguistic and digital terms. This type of immersion may create unease in the learner, but such unease can result in productive gaps wherein the learner may experience growth—again, both linguistic and digital. Developing linguistic and digital proficiency forms the basis for learning objectives and course design. Finally, this chapter will affirm that the core activity of DHL2 is designing and building multimodal products, regardless of the scale of inflection chosen.

DHL2 as a Strong Communicative Approach

In this section, we will examine "strong" communicative approaches to L2 instruction and how a DH-inflection (i.e., the valorization of digital humanities methods/approaches and incorporation of DH assignments/ projects) is a means by which to support or enhance a strong communicative approach in the L2 classroom through shared points of contact between the two—namely, the design of authentic and meaningful tasks that are highly communicative in nature. Diane Larsen-Freeman and Marti Anderson characterize content-based instruction as a "strong" version of the communicative approach because it "goes beyond giving students opportunities to practice communication. The strong version asserts that language is acquired through communication" (Larsen-Freeman and Anderson 2011, 131). Their proposal is that there are varying degrees of communicativeness achieved within permutations of the communicative method, depending upon the extent to which language and the act of communication are central and intrinsic to the pedagogical approach. In content-based instruction, the focus is not on grammatical practice but rather on using the language to explore a topic.

The shift from language-focused instruction to content-focused instruction offers a "strong" version of communicative course design because it renders all interaction therein practical and deeply entrenched in the needs for communication. Such interaction surpasses, for example, short role-playing activities in the L2 classroom designed to offer an opportunity for authentic communication that is momentary and ultimately simulated in nature. The use of collaborative DH activities and project-based work throughout a course that is integrated into the design and implementation across a semester permits rich interactions and opportunities to reflect on authentic and pragmatic language use. DH methods may be implemented across a range of proficiency levels to increase digital literacy while offering occasions for immersive content- and task-based learning. A valorization of DH methodology and its emphasis on localized and course-specific implementation (Mahony and Pierazzo 2012; Cordell 2016) informs course design in a way that complements the goals of content-based L2 instruction. By extension, DH projects offer productive opportunities for enhancing communicative activities through their immersive and engaging use of the target language to complete the project.

As Pitman and Taylor (2017) note, the points of similarity between DH and modern languages are numerous. Both disciplines are skills-driven, thrive from immersive practices, and offer a lens through which to examine a number of humanities disciplines, ranging from literature to art to history to linguistics. Take, for example, the French immersion program in Ontario, Canada. Students whose L1 is English may enroll in the French immersion program where all academic disciplines are taught in French with the exception of an hour of English each day. Content-based instruction is the norm because other than the hour of French language offered daily, students develop their language skills while learning other disciplines, including science, math, and history. This immersive approach parallels advanced language classrooms in higher education in the United States wherein literature and other subjects are taught in the target language. If humanities courses were inflected with digital humanities tools and methods across the curriculum, as Locke (2017) proposes in his description of Michigan State University's digital liberal arts initiative, Lab for the Education and Advancement in Digital Research, a similarly productive opportunity might arise for students to deeply engage with the digital. Second language students are poised to succeed in such an endeavor as it parallels their own immersive training.

Digital and Linguistic Immersion:
Play, Collaborate, Share

Another point of similarity is the immersive nature of L2 and DH instruction. Neither language learning nor digital humanities may be fully absorbed through a detached, passive engagement with the materials. On the contrary, the most successful approaches to both require a certain degree of immersion in the discipline. Where L2 learners often complete language labs, DH-inflected courses defy traditional conceptions of humanities courses by immersing the students in the tenets of the field, involving them in design and analysis as well as training learners to use the tools of the trade. In essence, approaches like that described by Harris (2013) evoke a strain of thought in DH pedagogy and practice that goes to the core of its nature: play and experimentation. It is described differently depending on the practitioner. Sayers (2011) asserts the importance of a "tinker-centric" approach in DH classrooms. Ramsay (2014) calls it "screwing around." This tendency toward experimentation and active engagement in DH-inflected classrooms complements the immersive, skills-driven, laboratory approach of many L2 classrooms.

It is perhaps here that the distinction between practice and pedagogy blurs, and where the true potential for DH-inflection in the L2 classroom emerges. Rather than setting oneself up as the authority in the room, thereby inherently privileging unidirectional communication with the instructor as the pinnacle of achievement because the instructor is the closest representative of the near-native or native speaker, a DH-inflected classroom acknowledges and values varying levels of experience and ability. While linguistically the instructor will be the most experienced in the room, each member of the class, including the instructor, is seen as an equal participant in a DH project, thereby modifying notions of authority and privileging multidirectional communication. Such a distinction underscores a truly communicative, student-centered classroom wherein a plurality of modes of discussion and participation is supported. At the same time, DH offers a more intentional means of engagement with a series of risks and rewards more characteristic of parascholastic interactions, be they in the professional realm or in the personal.

The DH-inflected classroom is a highly collaborative, skills-driven, and project-based space that privileges process over finite, terminal notions of completion as a measure of success. DH practitioners, particularly those who reflect on pedagogy in a meaningful way, recognize that workflow in DH may not always conform to the limitations of the semester, just as developing linguistic proficiency may not correspond neatly to conventional notions of language sequences. While contact hours may provide some general guidelines for acquiring linguistic proficiency ("Proficiency Targets" 2014), they are general at best and do not allow for individuation or variation among learners or even between skills ("How Many Hours of Instruction Do Students Need to Reach Intermediate-High Proficiency?" 2010; C. Cohen 2016; Tschirner 2016). DH-inflected courses require a thoroughly collaborative approach, drawing upon the tenets of cooperative language learning that emphasize teaching collaborative and social skills (Larsen-Freeman and Anderson 2011). Such an environment promotes "positive interdependence," meaning that students "are not thinking competitively and individualistically, but rather cooperatively and in terms of the group" (Larsen-Freeman and Anderson 2011, 189).

The benefits of such an approach are immediately apparent to L2 learners and instructors; cooperative work not only facilitates opportunities to develop "zones of proximal development" (Vygotsky 1978), it also promotes meaningful linguistic negotiation among speakers. The project-based approach to DH work permits groups to thrive in a focused, goal-oriented mode while accomplishing concrete, real-world tasks. They are not limited to role-playing in a fictional skit (not that there is anything wrong with role-playing; on the contrary, it may be used fruitfully in a wide array of levels to accomplish specific goals, including in the DHL2 classroom). However, a DH project by nature offers a range of modes of interaction and a variety of linguistic tasks that are at once personal and transferable to a professional context. For example, students must determine the objectives of the project, describe how they envision the digital project working, report back regarding progress, and ask and answer questions on subjects ranging from the personal (i.e., opinions on the project, timelines) to the abstract (discussions regarding design and implementation). This type of negotiation and shifting between tasks promotes proficiency as well as facilitates the student's confidence and control over material.

In addition to the practicality of a DHL2 approach, it is motivational as it presents a goal-oriented means of interaction with a clear purpose. This is where the selection of topics for DH projects is particularly important. Instructors should select projects and tasks that align with course topics and goals to promote an interested and engaged environment. For example, in an advanced French seminar on seventeenth-century French literature focused on travel, identity, and cartography, my students and I mapped the movements of one of the travel authors we studied, Jean Chardin, in order to get a feeling for the physical reality of travel in this period (the time it took, the distance traveled, the means by which one traveled) and the relationship between the text's structure and the geographical movements of the author. This tied in nicely to several course goals, including "to evaluate how identity and representation was constructed in seventeenth-century travel literature" and "to map digitally seventeenth-century works and compare these geographical representations with the structures of the texts themselves." Through such a process, learners gain a certain level of mastery that contributes to their ownership of both the material and the language. This type of multilayered activity provides fruitful opportunities for critical engagement and creative thinking. Additionally, it elicits production at a variety of levels, and DH activities (and the level of student responsibilities therein) can be scaled up or down to correspond to the linguistic and digital proficiency of the learners in conjunction with the learning outcomes for the lesson or course.

DHL2: Productive Unease and Linguistic Growth

DH utilizes technology as a means to an end, one determined by careful design and intentionality through which technology should (1) provide insight into the research question being asked (Unsworth 2002) and (2) result in a certain amount of "productive unease" as Flanders (2009) terms it—that is, a feeling of discomfort when traditional methods are confronted with new ones, but that lead to new insight because they cause one to question and reconfigure how one moves forward with the research question and calls attention to the nature of the mode of communication itself, be it a wiki or an interactive visualization. In a pedagogical context, this unease may be interpreted somewhat differently, particularly in terms of second language acquisition (SLA). In terms of SLA, this productive unease recalls the moment when, in interactionist theory, L2 learners become aware of gaps in their language use due to breakdowns in communication. These breakdowns occur during social interactions, and the pursuant negotiations of meaning help the learner to notice and internalize the input (Gass and Selinker 2008; Blake 2008). The corresponding "productive unease" in the DH-inflected classroom points to a propitious environment that encourages negotiation and reflection, a particularly beneficial space wherein to explore these gaps in a supportive, collaborative environment. In DHL2 classes, learners may cooperatively solve specific tasks while productively considering their language use and the gaps therein. Beyond the linguistic implications, such an approach perhaps implies greater risk than typically implied in the classroom setting, including questions regarding authority and authorship, workload and division of labor, and public versus private spheres of engagement that contribute to both the strength and the challenge of a DH-inflected approach to second language instruction.

Proficiency as a Framework for Learning Objectives

To implement DH methods into the L2 environment, the practitioner must mete out in equal portion a focus on design and structure. Thoughtful and attentive scaffolding of activities has long been a hallmark of L2 instruction, particularly with regard to the integration of realia, due to the nature of linguistic proficiency and acquisition (De Carlo 1998; Kreuger 2003; Bradley and Bradley 2004; Nance 2010; Rassaei 2014). Similarly, proponents of DH in the classroom find greater student success within a carefully structured frame. According to Harris, "students thrive in an atmosphere of discovery where they are allowed to intellectually explore particular areas of study with the help of an infrastructure put in place by faculty members" (2013, 5). I propose paralleling DH competency with the varying linguistic proficiency levels as designated by the American Council on the Teaching of Foreign Languages (ACTFL). The selection of task should correlate with the linguistic ability of the L2 learner in the respective level with an ultimate goal to progress to autonomy, both linguistic and digital.

In particular, we may capitalize on the classifications of novice, intermediate, and advanced proficiency as characteristic not only of linguistic proficiency but also of information and digital literacy. Introductory or novice DH topics, for example, would include consideration of public and openly accessible, digitally curated materials, allowing students to gain familiarity with a particular methodological approach. It would be appropriate for this level of learner to participate in the analysis of a digital curation project by contributing metadata (tags) or by preparing simple user guides for a general public. If learners are participating in the preparation of a digital gallery, they may contribute ideas regarding design and scope. Novice-level learners seek to gain familiarity with functions and best practices but may not yet master them.

Intermediate-level DH topics would include design and analysis of functionality with regard to digital tools as well as elaboration of the topics described in the novice step. Building on our example above, these students might participate in the creation of a digital curation project through the selection of materials or the delineation of parameters for inclusion using a specific tool identified by the instructor, such as Omeka, and relying on guidance from the instructor throughout. Learners at this level could be characterized by an imperfect, intermediate level of mastery (i.e., they may have a more fluid understanding of specific tools or methods to which they have been exposed but may lack autonomy when attempting new tasks). Intermediate-level DH users may contribute to the design and building of DH projects without needing to know how to code by using readily available DH tools, like Omeka, Scalar, or even WordPress.

Advanced-level DH users would be characterized by a certain degree of autonomy. They are aware of various techniques, able to clearly and accurately enunciate ideas about design and scope, and in possession of a certain facility in moving between tools and modality of use. This does not mean said transitions will be effortless or even error-free, but this level of DH user has a degree of autonomy not characteristic of lower levels of proficiency. It is not necessary that only advanced-level language learners pursue advanced-level DH tasks, but it may be difficult to implement them from a linguistic perspective in a lower-level classroom. Much will depend on the parameters of the project, the quantity of scaffolding, and the time available.

Levels of Engagement in DH-Inflections

Harris (2013) proposes three levels of DH that may be implemented, depending on the degree of engagement and time one might have as well as the learning objectives one wishes to accomplish. I have borrowed her levels but would propose that they be read as varying degrees of inflection of DH methodology into the L2 classroom, paralleling what we might term "weak, medium, and strong" levels of the communicative approach. Each of these varying manifestations of levels of engagement may be paralleled with the levels of implementation of the communicative approach outlined by Larsen-Freeman and Anderson (2011): that is, the "bloom-and-fade" activities represent a "weak" inflection of DH, the "assignment level" corresponds to a "medium" inflection, and the full course or multicourse exemplify a "strong" inflection of DH.

Bloom-and-Fade Activities as Weak Inflections of DH

Modeled on Bethany Nowviskie's category utilized for digital scholarship, Harris proposes this as a useful conception for single-day DH activities that are limited to the scope of a lesson: "By using bloom-and-fade strategies, faculty can implement a given tool during a class session without asking students to theorize its use, investigate its efficacy, or even interpret its cultural value. Bloom-and-fade is meant to be seamless but employ collaboration without turning the project into a multi-day or scaffolded assignment" (Harris 2013, 13). These small assignments contribute to learning objectives but may not constitute a substantive portion of the grade; rather, they are incorporated into other components. This level offers a limited introduction to DH methods and may be implemented at any level of linguistic proficiency. I propose this be considered a "weak" inflection of DH. These activities are ideal for those constrained by time and who wish to introduce DH to L2 learners in a productive and limited way.

Individual Assignment(s) as a Medium Inflection

At this level, students "employ emergent technologies to facilitate screwing around and play" (Harris 2013, 12). The focus is upon offering assignments that may represent a portion of the grade to allow a fuller consideration of DH. For example, a course may have a percentage of the grade allotted to the DH project (i.e., 10 or 20 percent of the final grade). This may incorporate multiple steps if properly scaffolded and is a great way to begin experimenting with DHL2. It offers entry into DH in a meaningful way without requiring the complete transformation of the course, making it effective at numerous linguistic proficiency levels. This approach would be characterized as a "medium" inflection of DH.

Full Course Implementation as a Strong Inflection

At this level, the entire course is scaffolded into various assignments that culminate in a final DH project. This represents a more comprehensive conceptualization of DH implementation and inflection, reflected both in the grade distribution and the overall course design. Such a course would include a range of dynamic engagements with DH. It might also still make use of traditional assignments but would integrate DH fully into the purview of the course. This approach exemplifies a "strong" inflection of DH.

Multicourse Implementation as a Strong Inflection

One level that is missing from the above categorization and from Harris's conceptualization is the multicourse implementation, which I would propose as a fourth possibility; that is, recognizing that a project may extend temporally beyond the bounds of the average semester, students from a course may contribute to a larger, multisemester project. Subsequent course offerings would build upon past semesters to move the project toward completion. This recognizes the reality of large-scale digital humanities projects that are completed on different timelines and often challenge the definition of "finished" (Kretzschmar 2009).

Each of these activities and course design options may be utilized independently, combined into the curricular design of a single course, or more deeply embedded into a language sequence or program as a whole. The advantage is that each of these levels of inflection allow flexibility in course design and implementation while still helping learners to build linguistic proficiency alongside digital literacy and readiness. Additionally, embedding different levels of DH inflection within L2 courses may enhance and strengthen the communicative approach utilized. For example, embedding a medium inflection of DH, like an individual assignment, may contribute to a strong communicative approach in a content-based course or a language acquisition course. There are a range of potential activities under the umbrella of the digital humanities, and practitioners are limited only by their own imagination.[1]

The advantage of such a classification is that it facilitates conceptualizing course design and the drafting of learning objectives. An instructor's goals will vary greatly based on the type of approach they select, and each of these levels permits a preliminary entry into DHL2 that may be customized based on individual need and level of proficiency. What should be clear from these levels, however, is the centrality of project-based work in DH inflections. Even bloom-and-fade activities implemented in a single class period may take up aspects of project work, whether it be an analysis of a digital product, a foray into creative design, or a discussion of how a traditional activity might be transferred into the digital realm.

Core Tenets: Designing and Building Multimodal Objects

Design and building are central and complementary tenets at the base of DH and may be experienced effectively at the novice and intermediate levels by capitalizing on extant digital tools (as described in the next chapter). To achieve advanced proficiency, it may be necessary to modify extant tools, depending on the complexity of the questions one seeks to answer. At this level, design and implementation on a larger scale might form primary points of inquiry and varying tools, like those used for text mining or geographic information systems (GIS) used for mapping. While one might capitalize on Harris's (2013) proposal that students serve as advisory board members and contributors on projects, advanced-level learners may wish to pursue introductions to programming and coding to permit personalization of materials. Keeping in mind definitions of digital literacy and digital readiness as being familiar with and able to use digital tools in a range of situations, I am proposing that using the tools and knowing how to find and design research questions form the primary points of inquiry rather than the primacy of coding. Nonetheless, it would be disingenuous to propose that programming and coding are not at all necessary. and many DH-ers do, in fact, learn one programming language or another, depending on their purposes (Python and Java are particularly popular).

The focus on a material cultures approach to digital objects both as the product of DH work and as the focus of study is a fruitful meeting point of DH and L2 pedagogy. Second language learners are often taught to engage critically with various realia, or authentic learning materials, to accomplish a range of tasks, be they linguistic or cultural, encouraging critical distance and reflective detachment while examining said objects (De Carlo 1998; Nance 2010). Similarly, the creation and examination of digital objects form a principal concern in the digital humanities (Harris 2013; Burdick et al. 2012; Cordell 2016; Mahony and Pierazzo 2012; Hirsch 2012). When considering the digital object, a number of attendant issues should be examined to better conceive the full import that digital literacy plays in today's culture (ACRL 2015). As Locke explains, "The critical evaluation of the 'digital-ness' of an object promotes a better use of the affordances of the media and information, while also understanding external implications, such as ethical and legal rights, privacy, permanence and impermanence, audience reception, and feedback" (2017, para. 23). These types of concerns echo and enrich the types of questions typically considered when examining authentic cultural materials in the target language.

The multiplicity of potential objects for examination and generation in the digital humanities recalls the multimodal nature of the discipline. While multimodal need not necessarily mean digital, as Virginia Kuhn (2016) reminds us (there are any number of analog examples, including newspapers that interweave image and text for varying purposes, be they informative or commercial), the digital realm tends to be multimodal as digital interfaces consider user-end experience and often offer interactive modes of use. In her "Multimodal" entry for the MLA Commons site, Digital Pedagogy in the Humanities, Kuhn notes the programmability inherent in digital multimodal works that adds another layer for potential meaning and expression to consider: "Once a word or a soundtrack or an image or a film is digitized, it becomes programmable and this, in turn, allows for a rich and nuanced integration of multiple semiotic modes into a single text. Thus, the affordances of the digital effectively expand the available semiotic resources, allowing communication and expression across the registers of word, sound, image, video and interactivity" (2016, para. 4). Kuhn calls for "multimedia literacy" and indicates that without learning fully to create and design or produce multimodal projects it is difficult to accurately understand and critique them, likening the process for gaining multimedia literacy to achieving proficiency in a foreign language (2016, para. 6), a particularly apt comparison for our purposes.

DH offers a complimentary means of focusing on digital and multimodal information literacy that may enhance the study and understanding of both the L2 and the digital reality of the target languages and cultures being studied but requires structured implementation. In the L2 classroom, a carefully scaffolded approach is warranted when using cultural objects like songs or films (Kreuger 2003). However, as Kreuger warns, and as is consonant with DH pedagogy (Mahony and Pierazzo 2012; Cordell 2016), selections of objects must be carefully made to enhance the learning objectives of the course without distracting from them. If we evaluate the digital tools and projects in the same structured and distanced way as we train our students to examine other cultural materials, we may get closer to understanding the multiplicity of cultural perspectives on the digital in a global context, thereby increasing awareness and understanding of target language digital culture and responding to calls to encourage a multiculturally and multilingually sensitive perspective in DH practices (Pitman and Taylor 2017; Liu 2012).

Summary

This chapter has explored the way in which a DHL2 program may be conceptualized. A DH-inflected course in the second language engages learners in a range of projects that require students to take on active roles evocative of the real-world tasks they will pursue in the professional realm. It may not be possible to exactly overlay the ACTFL proficiency guidelines with our own DH literacy guidelines. For example, one must consider the need for individualization, both in terms of programmatic and student need. Moreover, one should keep in mind that the institutional environment and available infrastructure will temper and impact curricular decisions. Nonetheless, it is possible and even recommendable to begin implementing a DH approach in novice language courses so long as the scope conforms to proficiency expectations. In the next chapter, we will explore implementing a DH-inflected L2 approach to course design and assessment while examining learner characteristics.

Reflection Questions and Activities

1. Why pursue a DH-inflected pedagogy in the L2 classroom? Outline the possible benefits and drawbacks.
2. What are the common, shared points between DH and L2 pedagogy? Can you think of additional shared points?
3. Define "productive unease" in both linguistic and digital terms.
4. Describe the varying proficiency levels proposed for DH-inflected courses. Imagine a possible activity for each level of proficiency and be prepared to share your ideas with classmates.

Recommended Further Reading

Flanders, Julia. 2009. "The Productive Unease of 21st-Century Digital Scholarship." *Digital Humanities Quarterly* 3, no. 3.

Harris, Katherine D. 2013. "Play, Collaborate, Break, Build, Share: 'Screwing Around' in Digital Pedagogy." *Polymath: An Interdisciplinary Arts and Sciences Journal* 3, no. 3. https://ojcs.siue.edu/ojs/index.php/polymath/article/view/2853.

Larsen-Freeman, Diane, and Marti Anderson. 2011. *Techniques and Principles in Language Teaching*. 3rd ed. Oxford: Oxford University Press.

Pitman, Thea, and Claire Taylor. 2017. "Where's the ML in DH? And Where's the DH in ML? The Relationship between Modern Languages and Digital Humanities, and an Argument for a Critical DHML." *Digital Humanities Quarterly* 11, no. 1.

Ramsay, Stephen. 2013a. "On Building." In *Defining Digital Humanities: A Reader*, edited by Melissa Terras, Julianne Nyhan, and Edward Vanhoutte, 243–45. London: Routledge.

———. 2013b. "Who's In and Who's Out." In Terras, Nyhan, and Vanhoutte, *Defining Digital Humanities: A Reader*, 239–41.

———. 2014. "The Hermeneutics of Screwing Around; or What You Do with a Million Books." In *Pastplay: Teaching and Learning History with Technology*, edited by Kevin Kee, 111–20. Ann Arbor: University of Michigan Press.

Sayers, Jentery. 2011. "Tinker-Centric Pedagogy." In *Collaborative Approaches to the Digital in English Studies*, edited by Laura McGrath, 279–300. Logan, UT: Computers and Composition Digital Press. http://ccdigitalpress.org/cad/index2.html.

Note

1. Battershill and Ross (2017) offer their own classification of DH activities according to class time required for implementation, and their classification may be of use to instructors considering varying designs (see in particular chapter 7). I find Harris's proposal (2013) useful in terms of course conceptualization and have proposed it accordingly.

3

Implementing a DHL2 Classroom: Design, Learner Characteristics, and Assessment

THE PARTICIPATORY, MULTIMODAL, and collaborative nature of DH pedagogy enhances the L2 classroom by offering opportunities for L2 learners to explore topics and themes related to the digital world and information literacy in both their L1 and L2 linguistic and cultural realities. This stance contributes to an expansion of the notion of the world-readiness standards (or five Cs) of foreign language education (Communication, Cultures, Connections, Comparisons, Communities). Through an emphasis on design and building, DH-inflected classrooms prepare students with critical thinking and analytical skills paired with an increased consciousness of and facility with the digital tools ubiquitous in today's global world. The global nature of the world, the awareness of the plurilingual and multicultural reality of existence, and the analytical distance gained from regular scaffolded interaction with L2 cultural materials make the DH-inflected L2 (DHL2) classroom a rich, productive space. This chapter will offer practical steps for implementation by exploring project-based design, learner characteristics, and general recommendations for workflow, evaluation, and feedback in DHL2.

Project-Based Design: Collaboration, Management, and Workflow

As is hopefully evident from the preceding chapter, there is a great deal of possibility in terms of DH inflection in the L2 classroom, ranging from single activities to full-length, multistep projects that take place over the entire semester or across multiple semesters. Within larger projects one may find a number of smaller activities designed to facilitate and enhance the learning process and scaffold the endeavor by providing the appropriate level of support depending on the learner's digital and linguistic proficiency levels. Given the predominance of project-based work in DH, it will be beneficial to describe this particular type of work, consider the necessary modifications to workflow, and examine how to manage the project-based DHL2 classroom. DH practitioners often describe their work as a series of projects, given the multimodal nature of output that does not necessarily conform to traditional nomenclature (i.e., monograph, article, etc.). Tabak (2017) and Burdick et al. (2012) propose the project as the most basic unit of DH practice. A DH project implies collaborative efforts (Tabak 2017; Burdick et al. 2012), either between fellow researchers (both within and beyond disciplinary boundaries) or between researchers and other types of contributors, including web developers or designers (Chan et al. 2017) and academic librarians (White and Gilbert 2016; Green 2016), to name but a few of the possible stakeholders in such processes.

DH projects are typically multimodal in nature and call for a critical framework to orient the user or reader and harness metadata to facilitate citation and searchability. They are characterized by the integration of text, image, sound, and video that often result in the creation of new knowledge and are typically openly accessible online, hosted on either an academic or a commercial platform (like WordPress). A significant amount of attention is focused on design (for example, the layout and integration of the various modes of media). Projects should offer introductions that not only explain the rationale but also consider and explain its implementation. Such introductions should also lead both the project's creators and its users to consider the role the technology itself plays in the communication of knowledge.

Project work is not new to the L2 classroom (Fried-Booth 2002), which makes it a particularly propitious means by which to integrate DH. As Fried-Booth asserts in her guide on the subject, project work is "student-centered and driven by the need to create an end-product. . . . The route to the end-product brings opportunities for students to develop their confidence and independence and to work together in a real-world environment by collaborating on a task which they have defined for themselves and which has not been externally imposed" (2002, 6). Fried-Booth describes three stages of project work: (1) the "planning stage" wherein the instructor works with students to determine the parameters of the project, its goals, and its design; (2) the "implementation stage" where students carry out various tasks related to the project objectives (this stage may or may not take place in the classroom); and (3) the "creation of the end product" stage where students collaboratively prepare the final product as planned in stage one (2002, 8). In this final stage, Fried-Booth indicates that evaluation and feedback may take place. She recommends developing a "follow-up programme" to discuss language needs that arose during the project (2002, 8). This is the same approach to project work that Larsen-Freeman and Anderson (2011) recommend in L2 contexts.

While this provides a useful framework for facilitating implementation of DH project work in the L2 classroom, it is important to note that DH project design and approaches to project work diverge from what Fried-Booth (2002) proposes. Where she notes that project work helps students to develop independence, the Scholar's Lab Charter recognizes explicitly the interdependency that characterizes DH work: "Our collaborations encourage inter-dependence. We prepare our collaborators to own their own projects, building confidence in their skills and avoiding over-dependence on expert staff. In doing so, we also teach effective collaboration through respect for the expertise and labor of all participants" (2016). The design of DH projects must be related to both programmatic and course learning objectives concretely and explicitly in order to clarify the roles and responsibilities of all participants in the project (instructor and students). Moreover, while projects should be broken into stages to allow for sufficient time to process and conceptualize the task (Antonioli and Cro 2018), the stages of project work described by Fried-Booth (2002) are evocative of linear conceptualizations that do not accurately represent workflow in the digital humanities, which tends to be more flexible in nature.

DH researchers recognize the inherent qualities of DH projects that distinguish them from more traditional forms of scholarship as "experimental, team-based, iterative and ongoing, rather than fixed or final" (Tabak 2017, para. 16). Edin Tabak (2017) proposes capitalizing on Agile software management processes to inform DH project management development. Agile stemmed from a reluctance, on the part of software developers, to maintain the linear, sequential phases of development proscribed through "waterfall methodology," which required completion of one stage prior to moving on to the next. Agile recognized that software development required greater flexibility to valorize interactions between customers (users) and developers. Iterative in nature, both Agile and DH projects recognize the need to move between stages in multiple directions depending upon the needs and specifications of the project. Tabak describes a flexible hybrid model prioritizing frequent communication among team members who have clearly demarcated roles. The life cycle of the project is characterized by continuous evaluation, permitting flexibility and adaptability. The DH project allows provisional closure that is open to subsequent innovation and intervention. Rather than linear and sequential, as Fried-Booth hints project work may be, Tabak's conception underscores the modular, flexible, and adaptive nature of project work that characterizes DH initiatives.

Learners in DHL2: Characteristics and Considerations

In this type of active, creative, and engaged methodology, the learner takes center stage as collaborator, designer, and researcher. This is a multifaceted set of responsibilities and roles that differ in complexity, agency, and scope from work in traditional language courses, making DHL2 a rewarding but demanding methodology. Inherent, however, is the need for a shift from students as consumers of digital media (Locke 2017) to students as generators. Such a shift underscores the primacy of reception in our interactions with the digital that are evaluated and challenged in DHL2 pedagogy. The benefit of such a change is not to be underestimated—rather than remaining locked into personalized, noncritical uses of technology, DHL2 encourages a critical, distanced evaluation of technology and a more nuanced understanding of its characteristics through active engagement with media as both consumers and creators. A particularly useful illustration of this shift is offered by Jentery Sayers in his study on tinker-centric pedagogy, prioritizing active modes of experimentation in conceptualizing digital pedagogy. Sayers characterizes students and instructors as "context-providers," wherein one "aims to create spaces that inspire or otherwise encourage others to contribute content" (2011, 293). Capitalizing on such an approach in a course of his own, Sayers notes that he and the students sought to create opportunities for new meetings of various media: "Our motivation was to repeatedly connect new technologies and media to tangible contexts, material situations, and off-screen issues, all toward seeing what exciting correspondences could be sparked in experimental, shared spaces" (2011, 294). In Green's evaluation (2016), this framework underscores the new forms of agency that DH students experience. This type of generative, active engagement is core to the learner experience in the DHL2 classroom.

An important ramification of students as creators is the question of ownership and credit, and the resulting unease students may feel when shifting into these new conceptions of their role in the classroom. Anderson et al. offer a unique perspective on this issue, writing as graduate students who noted the lack of scholarship dealing with this very question: "Much of the scholarship related to students in DH focuses on pedagogy . . . but very little deals with students as collaborators or active participants in the projects whose success depends, to a great degree, on their labour" (2016, para. 4). Their study finds that there is a discrepancy between faculty and student perspectives on labor and collaboration in DH projects. While faculty perceived that the projects were heavily collaborative in nature, students reported working individually for the majority of the time. They also noted that they had no formal training in the tools and technologies used for the project, leading to significant challenges as they moved forward. Ultimately, students' views did not correspond to faculty views on the collaborative nature of project work. These views may well stem from the inherent power balance within the academic structure. While rhetoric regarding collaboration reflects an ideal, Anderson et al. propose that it does not parallel the reality in which most find themselves: "The reality is that students do not share the same intellectual or social authority as their supervisors and other academics" (2016, para. 10).

These findings are concerning and merit examination here as we work toward establishing an inclusive DHL2 pedagogy. Both the University of California, Los Angeles (UCLA), and the University of Virginia (UVA) have offered statements guiding notions of workflow, collaboration, and rights for students in digital work. UCLA's Student Collaborators' Bill of Rights (Di Pressi et al. 2015) and UVA's Scholar's Lab Charter (Scholar's Lab 2016) underscore the importance of credit and equality as well as shared ownership over intellectual property produced in collaborative projects. Nonetheless, although there is significant discussion and awareness of this reality among faculty, there is a disconnect in student perception of the same, even when such documents are explicitly referenced and shared in the classroom setting (Antonioli and Cro 2018). Findings such as those laid out by Anderson et al. (2016) and Antonioli and Cro (2018) underscore the need to think carefully about balanced instruction that renders explicit the role students play in a project. While DH values "the social and collaborative production of knowledge over the ideology of the individual scholar" (Whitson and Whittaker 2013, 4), this value is lost if not reinforced pedagogically.

To address these concerns, Anderson et al. propose several excellent solutions: (1) formalize group structures so that tasks are distributed democratically and responsibilities/roles of all involved are clearly described; (2) build into the project timeline space and time for training and communication (they note that training is often seen as subordinate to the project rather than considered separately from a learning perspective; in this stage, they propose show-and-tells or lightning talks to share formally and informally progress on a particular aspect of the project or on training); (3) encourage student-led DH projects to promote student authority and ownership; (4) encourage student-led dissemination of work on larger DH projects in which they have participated; and (5) recognize and acknowledge the value of mentorship (termed "affective labor"). On this last point, Anderson et al. insist,

> Crucially, the exchange between speaker and audience is not monetary, but communicative: both parties invest in a sense of community-building, and the free and open exchange of knowledge. Mentoring is perhaps the single most important and sustainable form of training in DH, as students who benefit from these activities will be more likely to share their own expertise in a similar way. (2016, para. 35)

These findings underscore the importance of clearly delineated and expressed expectations in any DH assignment. Additionally, it is imperative to maintain frequent check-ins with students and between group members to anticipate any concerns.

Another key means by which to emphasize these values is by implementing frequent reflection activities wherein the instructor may touch base with students to check progress, determine workflow, and measure perceptions on labor. Thus, the instructor may modify the approach to the project as necessary to address student concerns throughout the course. This points to the importance of maintaining flexibility in course design and appropriately scaffolding all assignments (discussed in the following section). Additionally, explicit and clear assessment criteria, outlined in rubrics that are shared with the students and link directly with learning objectives for the course, are imperative to reducing unease and increasing transparency (discussed below).

One final point bears mentioning, and it relates to the question of student agency and the core tenet of sharing that runs through DH pedagogy. The UCLA Student Collaborators' Bill of Rights proposes that students be given the freedom to opt out of DH work, underscoring that students may not wish to participate in a public forum: "When digital humanities projects are required for course credit, instructors should recognize that students may have good reasons not to engage in public-facing scholarship, or may not want their names made public, and should offer students the option of alternative assignments" (Di Pressi et al. 2015, sec. 8). For any number of reasons, students may not feel comfortable with their name or identity being shared openly. This question resonates particularly in the K–12 setting. There are a few options to consider. One would be to offer students an alternative assignment. However, such a choice would negate the benefit a student would obtain from a DHL2 pedagogy and would ultimately become difficult for instructors to manage. Another possibility would be to create joint ownership of the project under the name of the class without specifying the individual members of the project. This would necessitate clarifying with students how they might claim ownership for the project in their résumés. For example, the instructor might recommend that students indicate that they were a member of the team responsible for the project, allowing those interested in claiming ownership to do so without infringing on the rights of those who prefer to remain private. Another option would be to work with students to discuss notions of authority and ownership, private and public, and consider together a solution that is amenable to all. For example, students might be encouraged to draft a contract that describes their ownership and how they would like to be credited. Ultimately, it will be up to the individual instructor to determine the best practice for the course; however, it is imperative to have this conversation with student collaborators, as it goes to the core of the methodology and is beneficial for students to consider. This is a particularly salient discussion to have as students begin to think about their online presence, one which will need to be curated carefully as they move into the workforce.

Flexibility, Reflection, Pacing, and Scaffolding in Activity and Course Design

Imperative in the classroom is a flexibility in approaching assignment and course design, and this is especially true of DH-inflected approaches to L2. There will be moments of frustration (Antonioli and Cro 2018) and unease

(Flanders 2009), stemming either from uncertainty about how to use the tools or from the unexpected outcomes of a particular DH engagement. Antonioli and Cro (2018) point to student nervousness over questions of authorship and ownership in their case study on implementing a DH approach in an advanced translation course as an important factor to consider in designing activities, suggesting that reflective activities focused on defining and claiming authorship may help alleviate some of this unease. Incorporating reflective activities is a crucial step in both DH and L2 pedagogy. These activities allow students to reflect on their own language use, their cultural awareness, and the impact digital tools or mediums may have on their understanding or construction of identity, both their own and that of target language speakers. Reflection encourages careful consideration of process and interior examination that is supportive of a growth mind-set (studied in further detail in the following section on assessment).

Equally important is adequately scaffolding activities, particularly in the L2 classroom. Since students are using their second language, instructors must provide or facilitate the acquisition of the practical vocabulary and linguistic strategies students will need to engage with various tools. Additionally, a gradual implementation of the tools as well as a critical consideration of them will be necessary to achieve the learning objectives of the DHL2 classroom. While this type of hybrid course is recommended by DH practitioners (Mahony and Pierazzo 2012; Cordell 2016), it could well lead to concerns regarding pacing (Antonioli and Cro 2018). Instructors in the DHL2 classroom might benefit from considering their role as indicative of a "knowledge broker," one who enables the "creation, sharing, and use of knowledge" and makes possible the dialogue between researchers and the public (Meyer 2010, 119; Chan et al. 2017, para. 5). Ultimately, the instructor facilitates this multidirectional process and models this type of interaction for students, training them how to successfully move between and, eventually, integrate DH and L2 practices. This is a practical skill as it is reflective of professional project management and will enhance student opportunities for professional development.

One area of concern that Antonioli and Cro (2018) point out is that of pacing. When integrating DH into the content-based L2 classroom, there is an inevitable challenge of managing the quantity of material presented and explored. It is important to recognize that DH offers significant benefits to students in terms of digital literacy, for example, but that developing said literacy takes time. Thinking critically about how to integrate DH into the learning outcomes for a course may help instructors to decide how best to proceed when designing the course. Additionally, capitalizing on a range of activities and levels of inflection are also fruitful ways of introducing students to pieces of DH methodology. It is advisable to break down DH work into distinct tasks, modeling for the students how they will manage their own project(s) or activities. DH values of collaboration and design may be considered from the very beginning of the class through exploratory activities evaluating various examples of digital media in the L2. Considering carefully the types of questions that will be imperative to the achievement of one's learning outcomes and working to insert those in varying modes and iterations throughout the course will help students to gain a clearer grasp on the methods involved with DH.

Localizing Assessment and Feedback

Just as DH projects are most effective when localized and relevant to students' studies (Mahony and Pierazzo 2012; Cordell 2016), so, too, must the means and criteria of assessment be specific and relevant. As Antonioli and Cro note (2018), there is a lack of model rubrics for evaluating DH and collaborative work in the L2 classroom. While Battershill and Ross (2017) do offer a few sample rubrics, their focus is on evaluating digital projects and does not deal with DH in an L2 context that presents its own set of challenges. This section will offer some practical advice for developing assessment practices that may be helpful as instructors individualize the approach to fit their own instructional style.

DHL2 valorizes formative assessment because it underscores the type of procedural and skills-building ethos at the core of its methodology, encouraging growth rather than punishing students for not already being savvy digital creators. As Viering (2016) notes, formative assessment "implicitly sets the expectation that students are not expected to know a particular overarching concept or skill from the get-go. By clearly outlining component concepts and skills and measuring progress as students master these intermediate components, formative assessment demonstrates that abilities can be developed and improved upon, a hallmark of having a growth mind-set." Assessment plays a crucial role in maintaining balance and clarifying expectations for students and instructors regarding workflow. Jody Shipka (2009) proposes that students participate in the assessment process by producing reflective statements. In said statements, they would evaluate their own choices and decisions regarding structure, content, design, and integration of media. This type of reflective statement is particularly beneficial in DHL2, not only from a linguistic perspective but from a growth perspective.

Nonetheless, assessing DH work can be challenging. Both Yancey (2004) and Green (2016) note that the multimodal nature of digital works renders assessment problematic. When developing criteria for rubrics and learning outcomes, a key consideration should be a project's readability and usability, stemming from the success with which students (either individually or as a team) are able to frame, contextualize, and integrate different modes of media (Ball 2004; Sorapure 2005; Green 2016). Rubrics, then, must reflect the multimodal nature of digital projects while considering desired outcomes for digital literacies (Green 2016). In DHL2, there is the additional consideration of the target language and the ramifications of intercultural communication to consider. In their case study, Antonioli and Cro (2018) propose holistic rubrics that reflect the student learning outcomes for the project, valorizing linguistic proficiency goals with statements that address qualities considered endemic to their conception of DH: professionalism, shared responsibility, collaboration, and respect for all participants and for multiple perspectives.

Just as assessment must be localized and explicitly linked to learning outcomes and course content, so, too, must feedback be specific. In formative assessment, the emphasis is on developing skills. Hence, constructive and clear feedback is particularly important to help students understand where they are in their progression. Given the project-based nature of DHL2, students need frequent, individualized, explicit feedback to succeed. This could take any number of forms, ranging from weekly check-ins to team or class meetings to daily evaluation and reflection activities. Varying the modality of feedback and underscoring reflection trains students to become reflective practitioners and supports a number of learning styles. The key to successful implementation of DHL2 is robust and frequent contact and feedback. Creating a supportive, positive environment wherein experimentation is the focus greatly reduces student anxiety and increases productivity.

Summary

This chapter offers recommendations for implementing DH methods in terms of course and assignment design. Flexibility, scaffolding, and reflection in DHL2 are key aspects of course design necessary to better prepare students to undertake project work and cope with student unease and concern regarding failure. Formative, localized assessments complement a growth mind-set and constructive feedback plays a crucial role in this process, as do explicit learning outcomes and rubrics whose criteria reflect clearly the project goals. Emphasis is laid throughout on process-oriented evaluation and design.

Reflection Questions and Activities

1. How does DH project work differ from Fried-Booth's conception of project work?
2. What shift is necessary in conceiving of the learner's role in DHL2? What challenges might stem from a DHL2 implementation in terms of learner experience?
3. What are the core characteristics of course design and assessment in DHL2?
4. Read over the **UCLA Student Collaborators' Bill of Rights** and the **UVA Scholar's Lab Charter**. Propose your own charter for use in your L2 classroom.

Recommended Further Reading

Anderson, Katrina, Lindsey Bannister, Janey Dodd, Deanna Fong, Michelle Levy, and Lindsey Seatter. 2016. "Student Labour and Training in Digital Humanities." *Digital Humanities Quarterly* 10, no. 1.

Antonioli, Kathleen, and Melinda A. Cro. 2018. "Collaborative Perspectives on Translation and the Digital Humanities in the Advanced French Classroom." *French Review* 91, no. 4: 130–45.

Cordell, Ryan. 2016. "How Not to Teach Digital Humanities." In *Debates in the Digital Humanities*. Edited by Matthew K. Gold and Lauren F. Klein. Debates in the Digital Humanities. Minneapolis: University of Minnesota Press. http://dhdebates.gc.cuny.edu/debates/text/87.

Di Pressi, Haley, Stephanie Gorman, Miriam Posner, Raphael Sasayama, and Tori Schmitt. 2015. "A Student Collaborators' Bill of Rights." Center for Digital Humanities, UCLA. June 8, 2015. http://cdh.ucla.edu/news/a-student-collaborators-bill-of-rights/.

Fried-Booth, Diana L. 2002. *Project Work*. 2nd ed. Oxford: Oxford University Press.

Green, Harriett E. 2016. "Fostering Assessment Strategies for Digital Pedagogy through Faculty–Librarian Collaborations: An Analysis of Student-Generated

Multimodal Digital Scholarship." In *Laying the Foundation*, edited by John W. White and Heather Gilbert, 179–204. West Lafayette, IN: Purdue University Press. https://doi.org/10.2307/j.ctt163t7kq.13.

Mahony, Simon, and Elena Pierazzo. 2012. "Teaching Skills or Teaching Methodology?" In *Digital Humanities Pedagogy: Practices, Principles and Politics*, edited by Brett D. Hirsch, 215–25. Open Book Publishers. https://www.openbookpub lishers.com/product.php/161/digital-humanities-pedagogy--practices--prin ciples-and-politics?161/digital-humanities-pedagogy--practices--principles -and-politics.

Scholar's Lab. 2016. "Charter." Academic. *Scholar's Lab at UVA* (blog). June 2016. http://scholarslab.org/about/charter/.

4

DH Tools and Examples: A Case Study through Cultural Comparison

IN THIS CHAPTER, I take a common activity in the L2 classroom at all levels and inflect it using various DH modes to probe the potential that a DH-inflected approach to L2 instruction represents. A core aspect of most L2 classes is the sustained and systematic examination of target cultures throughout the course. Even at the novice level, students are asked to consider the sociocultural and linguistic realities of the target language and cultures, stemming in part from the world-readiness standards (Five Cs) and their centrality in L2 instruction. A common activity in the L2 classroom is the comparison of aspects of the target cultures with one's own experiences and may be accomplished in a variety of ways, be they formal assessments or informal class discussion. This basic type of cultural comparison will form the focus of our exploration of tools and methods throughout the following section. I will describe several potential assignments and recommend tools that could be used to accomplish them. The activities and tools correspond to the characteristics identified above as central to DH methodology—public, open, collaborative, inclusive, and generative. In order to facilitate entry into DH for the nonspecialist, I have selected tools that are (1) free to use and easily accessible and (2) do not require advanced programming or coding skills to learn them, just a willingness to experiment and tinker.

Variations on the Cultural Comparison Theme:
Expanding the Language Community

A variation on the cultural comparison project, typically occurring as a class discussion oriented around a cultural note in the textbook, would have students design and conduct interviews with speakers of the target language both in the local community and abroad by digital means (email, video conferencing), be they native speakers (NS) or non-native speakers (NNS). Students would work collaboratively to compose interview questions, a step that could be modified depending on the level of the language learner and the learning objectives of the project (i.e., rather than a small-group assignment of prepare and report, it could be either instructor-led and worked on as a whole class or assigned as a homework assignment that students would then bring back and share in class discussion). Options for modes and types of questions to consider include (1) individual, personal information elicited in a survey-like form; (2) small group or one-on-one interviews conducted by the students with the NS/NNS; or (3) whole-class interviews with the NS/NNS invited to the class as a guest speaker (the latter being a particularly good option for K–12 environments). Students could collect this data, in the form of their own notes, survey results, and even videos if the interviewee is willing, and compile it for use in one of the DH activity manifestations that follow.

Researching a cultural topic by exploring the learner's own perceptions and opinions while comparing them to those expressed by NS and NNS of the L2 in the learner's local community helps learners gain a more varied and realistic view of the target language and culture both at home and abroad. An additional step might include supplementary research of the topic through both material and digital resources, offering an opportunity to compare the mediums through which the message is communicated and determine whether these discourses represent similar or widely divergent narratives in comparison with the individual experiences of the interviewees. While traditionally NS have been privileged in communicative approaches to L2 instruction, Compernolle and McGregor (2016) note that this concern with authenticity is reductive, idealized, and ultimately unrealistic. They propose a modification to the conception of the authentic speaker to extend beyond the idealized monolingual native speaker and include the speaker who "has appropriated patterns of language and meaning that are recognizable within and across communities of speakers of the language." They continue:

Learners do not become authentic by emulating perfectly an idealized native speaker of the language they are learning, but instead forge their identities as authentic speakers in multiple and variable ways that may align with, or diverge from, expected norms from one individual to the next, and from one context to the next. (Compernolle and McGregor 2016)

Thus, it would be appropriate for students seeking to examine the L2 community around them to interact with all L2 speakers, both NS and NNS, and learn from those experiences, perhaps even considering the impact of NS or NNS status on the perceptions of the cultural topics in question and the perceived authority with which said speaker deals with the topic.

Discovering and Sharing: Public and Open Discourses

In terms of the public and the openly accessible, the creation of websites or blogs wherein DH-ers may share the results of their work is an excellent starting point for entry into the digital humanities. Formalizing reflections on cultural lessons and involving students in discussions to share said reflections in a public forum in a professional and appropriate manner is an approachable and practical way to introduce students to some of the core components of DH methodology. For website design, **WordPress** is a very user-friendly platform for blogging that has been a popular and practical choice in DH. Built on a modified version of the open-source content management system named WordPress, WordPress.com is best known as a blog host and allows a great variety of design options while permitting multiple types of users to be assigned to a site, facilitating collaborative work. Another possible platform for web publishing is **Scalar**, a free, open-source web-based authoring and publishing tool developed by the Alliance for Networking Visual Culture. While Scalar does offer some great features because it is designed to capitalize on a digital, web existence and permits multiple users and roles, it is a more challenging interface and the instructor should experiment with it prior to selecting it. Antonioli and Cro (2018) outline some of the pros and cons involving Scalar in the L2 context.

These types of open, public projects offer an excellent basis for beginning discussions central to DH methodology, including preliminary considerations of building, design, scope, project management and participatory collaboration, and the nature of public discourse. Websites often form the basis for connecting DH projects with the public and the rest of the DH community, so it is fitting to begin with basics of digital publishing as it is a constant in DH outreach and presentation and immediately transferable to professional contexts. In our example activity (comparing cultural information and perceptions in L1 and L2 cultures), students could begin by describing a particular cultural practice studied in class. The description could take any of a number of forms, depending on the level of the learner, and could range from pictures and short phrases to paragraph-length descriptions to videos embedded using YouTube. The class would work cooperatively to design the site and determine the parameters of the assignment. These discussions should touch on the importance of accessibility in design for all users (Williams 2016). It might also be a good time to consider whether there are differences in designing websites for commercial, educational, or personal purposes (there are) and how said practices might differ or remain similar across varying cultural and linguistic contexts.

Wikis offer unique opportunities to capitalize on the cooperative production of knowledge in the L2 context that may challenge traditional notions of authority and focus on the individual learner's language production. A wiki is a "freely expandable collection of interlinked web pages, a hypertext system for storing and modifying information—a database, where each page is easily edited by any user with a forms-capable Web browser client" (Leuf and Cunningham 2001, 14). The main difference between a wiki and a blog is the way that information is organized; a blog is typically temporally structured (the most recent post is found at the top, regardless of topic or keywords) whereas a wiki is organized based on content (The College of Wooster n.d.). The most famous example is inevitably **Wikipedia**.

In the L2 context, Andreas Lund (2008) argues that the nature of work in wikis is interdependent, promoting collective zones of proximal development (ZPDs). In a case study examining a high school English as a second language class's preparation of a wiki to collect student-generated content around the theme, "Our USA," Lund notes that the nature of the activity contributes to enriching the L2 classroom through social and cooperative means:

> The broader, collective assignment requires that learners seek to link individual production to the dynamic and collective potential of the wiki. This involves trusting others to contribute productively and developing sensitivity towards the totality by relating one's own contribution to those of others, that is, we see the emergence of a collective ZPD. (47)

Wikis provide a fruitful combination of the core tenets of DH and L2 pedagogy. Capitalizing on the focus on web design and organization, wikis form a natural progression from the use of blogs and prepare students for a subsequent discussion regarding collective bibliographic management systems (below). Building on the assignment we described in the beginning of this section, a class could cooperatively select a cultural topic from their reflections, build a cooperative bibliography, and then draft a wiki on the topic. Laura Estill (2017) describes the use of the most famous wiki, Wikipedia, in an educational DH setting. In her article, she outlines an assignment where students in a Renaissance drama class research and prepare an entry on a play they adopt and study to contribute to Wikipedia. Estill affirms,

> Writing for Wikipedia in a literature classroom engages students to question the literary canon, to consider the role of editors and editions, and to undertake research using primary and secondary sources. As is often the case with writing Wikipedia articles, this research and writing helped students develop a sense of mastery of the material and provided exigence for real-world writing. (Estill 2017, para. 4)

Using Wikipedia in an educational context is not new; indeed, the **Wikipedia Education Program** encourages educators and students to contribute to Wikipedia.

Wikipedia plays an interesting role when considering authority and publishing in the ecosystem of knowledge. It challenges traditional notions of authority over knowledge by capitalizing on crowd-sourced contributions rather than privileging hierarchical constructions of knowledge as exemplified in traditional academic publishing ventures (Vandendorpe 2015). Additionally, because it is open and crowd-sourced, it is a much more responsive form of knowledge sharing (i.e., it is updated more quickly and perhaps more regularly). However, the same strengths may be its weaknesses. Updating and editorial standards are irregular because it is open and crowd-sourced. Many teachers warn against using the platform as an unreliable and unverified source of information. Nonetheless, it remains an important fixture in the ecosystem of knowledge, and students and the general public alike regularly rely on Wikipedia as a first entry into a given topic. It makes sense, then, to work to improve the information provided therein.

Second language classrooms could bring an interesting side to this type of assignment due to learners' multilingual abilities. Drawing again on our example project, students could compare entries in the L1 and L2 and examine what discourses are prevalent with regard to the same cultural topic and how those discourses shape the reader's understanding of the topic. Additionally, they could explore the use of Wikipedia in L1 and L2 contexts as well as stylistic tendencies exemplified therein before either drafting their own contribution or contributing to and enhancing an extant entry in both the L1 and L2.

DH methods render explicit the intentional use of technology but also demand reflection on the same. Fruitful discussion in the L2 classroom could ensue from the implementation of DH to further and better understand how these tools and their use figure into the L2 sociocultural digital landscape. Additional points for consideration would be how the use of the tools in the L2 classroom condition and frame the students' own interactions and understanding of material cultural of both the L1 and L2, enriching the imperative to compare L1 and L2 cultural contexts stemming from the world-readiness standards. This type of work would also contribute to a more nuanced understanding of target cultures, particularly when the majority of our students' interaction with them are mediated through digital means.

Collaborative Bibliography:
Critically Compiling Resources

An extension and enhancement of the cultural comparison and reflection activities I have described would be to introduce students to collaborative bibliographic management tools. In an analysis of student DH projects, Harriett E. Green (2016) found that they all shared strong introductions that provided an overview to the work as well as careful selection of media and accurate integration of the same into the project. However, there were widely divergent citational and metadata practices in the student projects, pointing to a need for more explicit instruction on that point in DH-inflected courses.

This is an area of particular strength for digital humanists, and one of the best and easiest-to-use free tools available is **Zotero**. Developed by the Corporation for Digital Scholarship and the Roy Rosenzweig Center for History and New Media, Zotero allows users to organize research easily into various libraries and folders. An extension for a variety of internet browsers is available, allowing users to add items to their libraries/folders with the click of a button while reading the item (articles, websites, blogs) in their browser. Through the web interface, users may create libraries and invite other users to them, allowing for collaborative research and facilitating the sharing of resources. The application does need to be downloaded, but the research citations and notes are backed up online, allowing users to access their libraries from different computers so long as they have an internet connection. It should be noted that the free version does have a cap of storage, but it is ample for most purposes, and users may download libraries/folders upon completing a project to free up space. Anecdotally, when my own students learned about Zotero in a workshop with our librarian, they were so thrilled that they began sharing the news with peers from across campus, and it transformed how they worked with bibliography throughout the class.[1]

Second language learners at all levels can benefit from learning about bibliographical and citational practices. Evaluating sources together as a class not only offers wonderful linguistic opportunities but also facilitates the development of digital readiness and proficiency, helping learners to determine the trustworthiness of digital and traditional sources. Building on the example activity where students might reflect on cultural readings in their textbooks, this type of personal reaction and reflection could serve as a preliminary step toward engaging with research on the cultural topics in question. Students could work together to determine the reliability of the sources and their relevance to the topic studied, and they could begin tagging sources—Zotero allows researchers to enter tags or keywords for each bibliographic entry, permitting the researcher to search for all articles that have those tags at a later time. This would lead naturally to the question of keywords and metadata.

Metadata is a necessary step in digital work to permit searchability. Information available online must be tagged appropriately with keywords that describe the content, thereby allowing it to be discoverable by search engines. **Twitter** hashtags provide a great starting point for this discussion, and the length and content of tweets makes this a possibility for all levels of language learners and may even enhance lexical acquisition. In our example activity, students could explore what Twitter hashtags are associated with a particular cultural topic in both the L1 and L2, creating a sample lexicon to study or analyze.

Analyzing and Visualizing Linguistic
and Cultural Materials

While the aforementioned activities exemplify the core concepts of DH in a user-friendly and accessible way, there are specific modes of activity that stem from digital humanities research initiatives. In particular, we will consider the most dominant categories of activities: text mining (and, by extension, analytics), mapping, and visualization more generally. Text mining and analytics are the use of computational methods to analyze characteristics of the text like word frequency and stylistic qualities. The most extensive use of text mining is exemplified recently in projects that explore distant reading, a macroscopic focus on large-scale literary analysis. Coined by Franco Moretti, the expression "distant reading" refers to Moretti's assertion that close reading may not allow researchers sufficient data to fully evaluate large questions like genre or respond to inquiries across long stretches of time, so researchers should focus on "distant" approaches, thereby broadening notions of the literary canon; most recently, this means harnessing computational models and software to "read" and evaluate the texts (Moretti 2013).[2]

A number of digital tools, in varying levels of sophistication and usability, are available for text mining, depending on the purposes of the user. One that is particularly easy to use is **Voyant Tools**. This "web-based reading and analysis environment for digital texts" was developed by Stéfan Sinclair and Geoffrey Rockwell. To use Voyant, the user must either have a text that is already machine readable (transcribed into digital format) or have a URL to insert so that Voyant can "read" a website. Using the tool is relatively simple and produces a range of data very quickly, including word frequency lists and visualizations of word distribution. Voyant offers a snapshot of the text, including word clouds and word frequency charts, transforming the text into graphic visualizations that challenge linear perspectives on reading and give students a taste of various approaches to texts or corpora such as those used in distant reading, corpus linguistics, and lexical and semantic analysis.

An added benefit of Voyant is that you may change the language so that the interface reflects the target language rather than English. This provides a wonderful opportunity to acquire new, specialized vocabulary in a highly visual and interactive way. Boyle and Hall (2016) have capitalized on Voyant in their advanced Spanish-language course on *Don Quixote* with positive results. Drawing on our example cultural reflection and research activity, students could feed the answers from their interviews, data collection, and/ or Wikipedia entries on selected cultural topics into Voyant to see whether or not specific terms or phrases were particularly frequent. Different levels of language users might find different aspects of Voyant useful; instructors of beginning language courses might ask students to distinguish between different categories of words and reuse them in their own sentences, while intermediate-level learners might be asked to share their thoughts on word frequency and discuss the word cloud that visualizes said frequency. Comparative analysis of results might also prove beneficial—for example, what conclusions may we draw from the words privileged by one speaker or another? Do these lexical choices proceed from a sociocultural milieu, or are they linked with gender, geographical identity, and so on? Tools like Voyant render visible what might go unnoticed otherwise.

Visualizations, or graphic representations of data, are a principal domain of interest to DH. As thinking around texts shifts away from linear emphasis, so do questions regarding spatial representation. Multimedia has done a great deal to influence and shape information in new ways, encouraging scholars to consider whether the research questions and results should be equally reshaped. David McCandless offers an illuminating TED Talk wherein he exemplifies the power of data visualization (McCandless 2010), and numerous examples are available on his website (McCandless n.d.). Within this category we may find projects involving mapping, in both a literal and more figurative sense.

Spatial Relations and Mapping

The use of geographic information systems (GIS) to evaluate spatial and logistic aspects of humanistic inquiry has become increasingly important in recent years. One of the global leaders in GIS is Esri, the international company that developed **ArcGIS**, a powerful GIS used to create maps and evaluate or analyze geographic data. While Esri does provide free ArcGIS bundles to K–12 schools and many universities do have software licensing rights available to the campus community (one should check with one's geography department for more information), ArcGIS does require training to be used effectively and may exceed the needs for introductory or intermediate projects in the L2 classroom. A simple entry into mapping, geotagging (the process of adding geographic metadata to media), and spatial awareness would be to use Google Maps. Google Maps is relatively user friendly, free, and allows novice users to get involved with mapping right away. On Google Maps, users can drop pins with information regarding various locations including photos and data, as Clarissa Clò describes in her Italian classes (2016).

Drawing on a subdiscipline of GIS, Hildebrandt and Hu (2013) describe an interdisciplinary approach capitalizing on multimedia mapping. They used Google Maps Application Programming Interface (API)[3] to generate an interactive, multimedia, linguistic map of Nepalese dialects and embed it in the online atlas designed for their project to map endangered indigenous languages in Nepal (Hildebrandt and Hu 2013; Hu 2017). One of the goals of the project was to prepare pedagogical materials for language instruction, and the project uses data from Google Maps combined with the research team's own field data, including photos and interviews, to create an interactive and usable map of the endangered indigenous languages. The map was then embedded into a website that included information about the team (including undergraduate and graduate student researchers), the research, and the results.

While Hildebrandt and Hu's atlas (2013) would qualify as an advanced DH project (or, again drawing from ACTFL proficiency guidelines, a superior-level project given the coding required for their particular iteration), the mechanics of the activity itself could be scaled back to accommodate a variety of language levels. For example, students in a beginner or intermediate-level language course could use Google Maps to track their cultural readings or the interviews they conduct with NS and NNS of the target language, providing an expanded conception of the L2 world and its participants for students. Alternatively, students could work together to write interview questions, conduct interviews in small groups, and compile the data they collect in a spreadsheet, each question corresponding to a column and adding location coordinates to permit layering.

The basis of many mapping and visualization projects is the spreadsheet. A spreadsheet is, essentially, a simple database. Using either Excel or Google Sheets, students may break down their results in a data form that may then be uploaded either to Google Maps or to a visualization utility like Palladio (described in the next section). The geographical location of each interviewee could be mapped using coordinates corresponding to their current location, for example, or to where they learned the language, or those locations that have special significance for the interviewee with regard to the cultural topic being discussed.

Such a project would provide a picture of language use in the community that is both immediate and impactful. This process could be extended across languages to get a picture of the plurilingual community in which students live. Additionally, students could decide whether and what types of multimedia they would like to incorporate in their map as well as identify potential resources for users of the map. The depth of detail and the types of questions, cultural topics, or data students collect may be modified depending on linguistic proficiency and may be selected to correspond to extant curriculums (for example, using cultural readings from the textbook as a starting point). Multimedia mapping allows for a degree of interaction that is particularly engaging while also calling into question the nature of the object itself—questions to consider with students as the map is designed and constructed.

Visualizing Data, Storytelling Tools, and Promoting Productivity

Another excellent, freely accessible toolset for visualization and data analysis that also allows mapping (among other things) is **Palladio**. Developed by Stanford University, Palladio is a web-based application that allows users to upload their data (typically in "tabular form," i.e., a spreadsheet; the site offers tips on preparing said spreadsheets) and Palladio goes to work. Users may either map coordinates, analyze relationships graphically, or prepare timelines and may even embed external links to enrich the data. One caveat—Palladio will not store work. It will allow users to download a project as a .json file (a form of Java) that will need to be reuploaded and resaved with new changes in subsequent iterations. Nonetheless, it is a powerful set of tools that gives users an opportunity to visualize their data in new and unexpected ways. Some of the best examples of Palladio projects are those connected with the larger project that generated the toolset itself, the **Mapping the Republic of Letters** project out of Stanford ("Mapping the Republic of Letters" n.d.), a large, multi-institutional project set examining the social networks of scientists and intellectuals from 1500 to 1800 and providing insight into the communication of ideas in Europe during the early modern period (see, for example, Comsa 2017).

In terms of use in class, working with Palladio would need to be done communally, and if an individual user made changes to the core file, they would need to save a new version. However, it is recommendable to work with these types of visualization tools in class. I have found that students thrive in a supportive environment wherein they may ask questions of the instructor as they experience new technology. In a pedagogical setting, the process of designing in Palladio would still remain a highly collaborative endeavor, and students might switch off as group leader on different days as they utilize the tool to explore their datasets, further contributing to a student-centered classroom modeling shared authority, ownership, and authorship.

Another internet-based, user-friendly visualization utility is **RAWGraphs**. Designed by the DensityDesign Research Lab (Politecnico di Milano), RAWGraphs is an excellent option to explore visualization. Users may upload a spreadsheet and then explore various types of charts to represent visually the data compiled in the file. The process of selecting the type of chart allows users to explore the question of data visualization, noting which methods are most effective for representing the information they seek to share. Charts are customizable and may be downloaded and saved on one's own computer. This utility can be particularly useful when visualizing datasets with multiple variables as it allows the user to tease out the potential of the data itself.

Visualization is, at its core, an opportunity to communicate information regarding the data one has collected in a compelling form. Another means for effectively sharing information are the **storytelling tools** made by Knight Lab at Northwestern University. Two particularly user-friendly tools are **StoryMapJS** and **TimelineJS**. StoryMap allows the user to overlay information on a map or a large image, creating a content-rich, interactive, multimedia interface. TimelineJS allows users to create interactive, multimedia timelines. The basis for each of these utilities is the spreadsheet, and these tools interface directly with Google spreadsheet, making working collaboratively feasible.

Facilitating all this work are various free, web-based productivity tools that enhance organization and task management. Google has a full suite of open, free office applications that are shareable and allow multiple users to interface synchronously with ease (**Docs** for word processing, **Sheets** for spreadsheets, and **Slides** for presentations). Google Docs is particularly useful for cooperative writing given that users may comment and chat within the app itself. Google Sheets allows users to share data and organize it easily with the same chat ability as in Docs. For presentations, in addition to Google Slides, users could also experiment with **Prezi**, an adaptive online presentation tool that allows team collaboration. To share and organize tasks for large projects, **Trello** is a particularly good and user-friendly choice. A web-based project management application, Trello allows users to create lists of tasks with dates/deadlines and notes. Users may also invite others and share the project lists with other users, and all may contribute and edit the task lists.

Variations and Scaling

Drawing on our proposed example, inspired in part by Hildebrandt and Hu's atlas (2013), we can imagine a DH project that could be implemented at various levels of linguistic and digital proficiency across the curriculum, and even shared across languages. Through a more inclusive and expansive conception of authenticity that values learner experience (Compernolle and McGregor 2016), students may explore the L2 community surrounding them as immediate and valid. Students may work collaboratively to design their project, select the media to include, conduct their interviews, compile their resources, and share their results. Mapping and visualization tools permit students to examine their results and gain insight into data collection and the implication of the same in profoundly impactful ways. Through DH tools, students may facilitate workflow, compile and evaluate results, and share new knowledge widely and openly, creating new opportunities for learners to gain expertise, agency, and authority.

A possible extension would be to combine this methodology with interviews conducted via Skype with speakers in other locations, either in target language communities or in other national or global language learning communities. This could easily be converted into a multisemester or multiyear project to which each iteration of students could contribute, checking in on former interviewees and adding to the database to provide a longitudinal view of multilingualism in the local language learner's community. The larger implications of such a study might point to considering the hegemony of English or the degree to which certain languages have increased in frequency in various geographic areas. The project allows students to contribute in meaningful ways, both in terms of how to design the research and how to build the ultimate results. Learners determine which characteristics they find most appealing in the design of their interview questions. Additionally, to maintain the localization imperative to successful implementations of DH, the information sought should be related to course topics. For example, most beginning- and intermediate-level textbooks have a range of cultural notes that could form a starting point for this type of project.

This type of multimodal, multistep project could be scaled up or down depending on the strength of inflection the instructor seeks to implement in the course design. Modes of input could be varied as well. Rather than students conducting interviews outside of class, the interviewee could be invited to the class. As a further variation, rather than conducting the interview orally, surveys could be generated and sent to collect the data using **Google Forms** or **Survey Monkey**, which does have a simple version of the software available for free. Alternatively, interviews could be filmed to provide a further layer of multimodal input to consider and include in the project. The data, whatever form it ultimately takes in one class, could form a rich subject of study for subsequent classes to consider and would introduce students to research and data collection in the L2 in a useful and meaningful way, encouraging a process of lifelong learning.

Summary

This chapter described how to take a typical activity in the L2 classroom (cultural comparison between L1 and L2 cultures) and inflect it using DH methodology. A range of freely accessible tools were described, as were a number of different approaches capitalizing on core activities in DH: designing, building, compiling, collaborating, visualizing, and mapping, to name a few. We illustrated how to scale activities depending upon the digital and linguistic proficiency level of the learner as well as the degree of inflection the instructor seeks in the implementation. Following the discussion questions, I have included a few sample DH projects to help illustrate the possibilities.

Reflection Questions and Activities

1. Have you ever used any of the tools mentioned? Which ones? In what context?
2. Which of the approaches/tools described seems most consonant with your current methodology?
3. Which tool seems to have the lowest learning curve in your opinion? The highest? Explain.
4. For each tool outlined, go online and tinker with it. Then, after examining the sample DH projects below, provide an example of how you might implement three different tools in your L2 classroom.

Sample DH Projects

"The Comédie-Française Registers Project." n.d. Accessed June 11, 2018. http://cfregisters.org/.

Hu, Shunfu. 2017. "The Manang Languages Project Atlas." The Manang Languages Project. 2017. https://mananglanguages.isg.siue.edu/atlas /#openModal.

"Mapping the Republic of Letters." n.d. Accessed June 18, 2018. http:// republicofletters.stanford.edu/.

Recommended Further Reading

Boyle, Margaret, and Crystal Hall. 2016. "Teaching 'Don Quixote' in the Digital Age: Page and Screen, Visual and Tactile." *Hispania* 99, no. 4: 600–614.

Clò, Clarissa. 2016. "Inventing the New Renaissance Generation: The Digital Humanities in FL Classroom through Visual Storytelling, Student Curation and Geospatial Scholarship (SWALLT Keynote 2016)." Presented at Southwest Association for Language Learning Technology, San Diego, April 1. https:// drive.google.com/file/d/0Bzh-ABZrF10qVXNsejlOakZ3eDA/view?usp =sharing&usp=embed_facebook.

Compernolle, Rémi A. van, and Janice McGregor. 2016. *Authenticity, Language and Interaction in Second Language Contexts.* Bristol: Multilingual Matters. https://books.google.com/books?id=5rbQCwAAQBAJ&printsec=frontcover #v=onepage&q&f=false.

Hildebrandt, Kristine A., and Shunfu Hu. 2013. "Multimedia Mapping on the Internet and Language Documentation: New Directions in Interdisciplinarity." *Polymath: An Interdisciplinary Arts and Sciences Journal* 3, no. 3. https:// ojcs.siue.edu/ojs/index.php/polymath/article/view/2842.

Kreuger, Cheryl. 2003. "Humanizing Language Courses with Technology, Songs, and Film." In *Teaching with Technology,* edited by Lara Lomicka and Jessamine Cooke-Plagwitz, 56–64. Boston: Heinle.

McCandless, David. 2010. "The Beauty of Data Visualization." Presented at TEDGlobal, Oxford, July 2010. https://www.ted.com/talks/david_mccandless _the_beauty_of_data_visualization.

Vandendorpe, Christian. 2015. "Wikipedia and the Ecosystem of Knowledge." *Scholarly and Research Communication* 6, no. 3. https://src-online.ca/index .php/src/article/view/201.

Notes

1. Working with your institution's library and librarians leads to invaluable resources. Many thanks to Sara Kearns of Kansas State University Libraries for her dedicated work with the students in FREN 711 in spring 2018; her careful demonstration of Zotero and discussions with the students regarding their digital humanities projects were invaluable activities that truly set the students up for success.

2. Ted Underwood (2017) argues that distant reading stems from a different intellectual tradition than digital humanities and is not in favor of conflating the two disciplines as inherently one and the same. While I do not propose to equate distant reading with digital humanities, one cannot help but recognize that developments in DH have aided work in distant reading, and vice versa.

3. Google Maps Application Programming Interface (API) is no longer available in the same way. In spring 2018, Google announced the arrival of Google Maps Platform, a streamlined one-stop-shop for API products available on a subscription basis for commercial purposes.

Conclusion

Challenges and Considerations
of a DHL2 Methodology

IN THIS BOOK, we have explored the digital humanities and the potential inflecting the L2 classroom with DH represents methodologically for informing a strong version of communicative language learning. The benefits are many, ranging from increased digital readiness and literacy to gaining highly transferable design, building, and collaboration skills that will set students up for success in their future careers. The author of this book hopes to have conveyed the possibility the digital humanities represent for L2 instruction, namely as a highly engaging, project-based, cooperative and social mode of learning. The focus on sharing and the public allows students, regardless of whether or not they study abroad, to visualize themselves as members of a larger language community that extends beyond the boundaries of the classroom. Through a DHL2 approach to learning, students work on real, necessary tasks deeply entrenched in the fabric of their L1 and L2 communities, facilitating their transition from local to global citizens.

Despite all the promise, the digital humanities have their detractors. In a recent article in the *Chronicle of Higher Education*, Timothy Brennan raises serious doubts as to the merits and import of the digital humanities, characterizing the field as "a wedge separating the humanities from its reason to exist—namely, to think against prevailing norms" (Brennan 2017). Brennan critiques DH practitioners for being long on optimism and short on critical interpretation or analysis. Eric Weiskott, in response, argues that digitization inevitably leaves its mark on the field. In a particularly powerful analogy, he proposes that it would have been absurd to affirm the primacy of scrolls over print culture at the development of the printing press; so, too, must we recognize that the digital age will condition and influence our research and our humanistic endeavors (Weiskott 2017). As Marshall McLuhan reminds us, the medium is the message. How we convey and receive information is inevitably tempered by the mode of conveyance. Weiskott is right, the digital is inevitable, and this is not really news; instructors have been dealing with technological distractions in the form of cell phones and laptops as well as benefiting from digital advances in terms of increased productivity and workflow management in the classroom for years. One may either rail against the digital move in the humanities, as Brennan is proposing, or engage it critically.

A critical engagement necessitates evaluating both the pros and the cons. One should not overlook the challenges that arise in pursuit of a DH-inflected L2 classroom. A primary consideration is financial. Instructors inevitably work within the realm of the institution with which they are affiliated, be it public or private, secondary or post-secondary. The fiscal reality is that there may not be the resources available to pay for dedicated servers or subscription-based software. Some software programs that require subscriptions may provide educational offers that allow teachers and students to use a version of the software for free (this is the case, for example, with ArcGIS). These considerations make the selection of tools particularly salient, so priority has been given to freely accessible, online tools that do not put an undue burden on an instructor seeking to adopt the methodology within a limited institutional infrastructure. It will be up to the individual instructor to determine what tools work best given their institution's financial situation.

From a linguistic perspective, there is a practical challenge in implementing DHL2 that bears consideration—many DH tools are developed and programmed in English by default, meaning that teachers interested in using a tool may be faced with an English-language interface. While such a reality does provide an important opportunity for discussing global accessibility and linguistic standards in the digital realm, the immediate question is how to proceed. One option is to seek out tools that allow users to change language settings. A number of tools do offer this ability, so learners could interact with the tool using the L2. For example, Voyant allows users to change languages, as does WordPress. This presents the added challenge of teaching a new vocabulary to students and creating vocabulary lists but would be highly beneficial in helping students to obtain a technical and practical lexicon. If the tool selected does not allow changing language settings, one might consider what this means in terms of accessibility for a language community. Advanced courses might consider undertaking a translation project to provide a guide to the tool in the target language. Alternatively, the class might work to generate its own user guide for a tool as part of their regular interactions with it.

Another challenge is finding and using DH tools. Fortunately, there are a wealth of resources available online; however, those resources change as technology develops, and funding sources fluctuate. For example, the Digital Research Tools (DiRT) Directory was a database that facilitated the selection of tools, and the developers were working to offer a Spanish-language translation of the database, indicating an awareness of the need for languages other than English to be represented. Supported by the Andrew W. Mellon Foundation, the DiRT directory categorized tools based on functionality, cost, and ease of use. However, the project that housed the directory originally, Project Bamboo, was eliminated, leaving the directory to be maintained by community users. The instructor interested in learning more about DH tools might consider consulting the website **The Programming Historian**, which offers a comprehensive set of tutorials on an array of digital humanities tools and techniques that are clear and very well done. These types of resources greatly facilitate the implementation of a DHL2 methodology.

The digital humanities offer a renewal of engaged, participatory modes of learning that can enhance what is already being done in the humanities classroom in general, and in the second language classroom in particular. The digital does not replace the humanities but rather offers an opportunity to critically engage and enhance humanistic inquiry. It is but one of any number of possible frameworks through which humanists explore their discipline. It is not meant to replace traditional approaches that utilize close reading any more than a DH-inflected pedagogy should replace the communicative approach in the L2 classroom. What DHL2 pedagogy *can* do is enhance communicative and meaningful language learning by helping students to fully engage in discourses in the field in an immediate way. This in turn permits learners to capitalize on their learning and develop their proficiency actively and professionally in a range of contexts that are transferable to a number of milieus upon completion of the course. Furthermore, from an institutional perspective, a DHL2 allows visibility and a public presence that allows instructors and students to underscore the importance of the discipline, particularly in times of limited budgets. Ultimately a DH-inflected second language classroom promotes the development of lifelong language use. DHL2 increases opportunities for interactions with language communities outside the classroom and that, in the end, is truly the goal of all language instructors.

Appendix: List of Digital Resources

Digital Resource	URL
ArcGIS	https://www.arcgis.com/index.html
Danteworlds	http://danteworlds.laits.utexas.edu/
Emotions of London	https://litlab.stanford.edu/LiteraryLabPamphlet13.pdf
Google Docs	https://docs.google.com/document/u/0/?tgif=d
Google Forms	https://www.google.com/forms/about/
Google Maps	https://www.google.com/maps
Google Sheets	https://www.google.com/sheets/about/
Google Slides	https://www.google.com/slides/about/
Mapping the Astrée	https://mappingastree.weebly.com/
Mapping the Republic of Letters	http://republicofletters.stanford.edu/
Palladio	http://hdlab.stanford.edu/palladio/
Prezi	https://prezi.com/
The Programming Historian	https://programminghistorian.org/
Quantitative Formalism	https://litlab.stanford.edu/LiteraryLabPamphlet1.pdf
RAWGraphs	https://rawgraphs.io/
Scalar	https://scalar.me/anvc/scalar/
StoryMapJS	https://storymap.knightlab.com/
storytelling tools	https://knightlab.northwestern.edu/projects/
Survey Monkey	https://www.surveymonkey.com/
TimelineJS	http://timeline.knightlab.com/
Trello	https://trello.com/home
Twitter	https://twitter.com/
UCLA Student Collaborators' Bill of Rights	https://humtech.ucla.edu/news/a-student-collaborators-bill-of-rights/
UVA Scholar's Lab Charter	https://scholarslab.lib.virginia.edu/charter/
Voyant Tools	https://voyant-tools.org/
Wikipedia	https://www.wikipedia.org/
Wikipedia Education Program	https://outreach.wikimedia.org/wiki/Education
WordPress	https://wordpress.com/
Zotero	https://www.zotero.org/

Bibliography

ACRL. 2015. "Framework for Information Literacy for Higher Education." Association of College & Research Libraries. February 9, 2015. http://www.ala.org/acrl/standards/ilframework.

Allison, Sarah, Ryan Heuser, Matthew Jockers, Franco Moretti, and Michael Witmore. 2011. "Quantitative Formalism: An Experiment." *The Stanford Literary Lab Pamphlet Series* 1 (January): 1–29.

Anderson, Katrina, Lindsey Bannister, Janey Dodd, Deanna Fong, Michelle Levy, and Lindsey Seatter. 2016. "Student Labour and Training in Digital Humanities." *Digital Humanities Quarterly* 10, no. 1.

Antonioli, Kathleen, and Melinda A. Cro. 2018. "Collaborative Perspectives on Translation and the Digital Humanities in the Advanced French Classroom." *French Review* 91, no. 4: 130–45.

Ball, Cheryl E. 2004. "Show, Not Tell: The Value of New Media Scholarship." *Computers and Composition* 21, no. 4: 403–25. https://doi.org/10.1016/j.compcom.2004.08.001.

Battershill, Claire, and Shawna Ross. 2017. *Using Digital Humanities in the Classroom: A Practical Introduction for Teachers, Lecturers, and Students.* London: Bloomsbury Academic.

Bennett, Sue, and Karl Maton. 2011. "Intellectual Field or Faith-Based Religion: Moving on from the Idea of 'Digital Natives.'" In *Deconstructing Digital Natives: Young People, Technology, and the New Literacies*, edited by Michael Thomas, 169–86. London: Routledge.

Berra, Aurélien, Claire Clivaz, Sophie Marcotte, and Emmanuelle Morlock. 2018. "Introduction." *Digital Humanities Quarterly* 12, no. 1.

Blake, Robert J. 2008. *Brave New Digital Classroom: Technology and Foreign Language Learning*. Washington, DC: Georgetown University Press. http://ebook central.proquest.com/lib/ksu/detail.action?docID=547784.

Boyle, Margaret, and Crystal Hall. 2016. "Teaching 'Don Quixote' in the Digital Age: Page and Screen, Visual and Tactile." *Hispania* 99, no. 4: 600–614.

Bradley, Karen Sue, and Jack Alden Bradley. 2004. "Scaffolding Academic Learning for Second Language Learners (TESL/TEFL)." *The Internet TESL Journal* 10, no. 5. http://iteslj.org/Articles/Bradley-Scaffolding/.

Brennan, Timothy. 2017. "The Digital-Humanities Bust." *The Chronicle of Higher Education*, October 15, 2017. http://www.chronicle.com/article/The-Digital -Humanities-Bust/241424.

Burdick, Anne, Johanna Drucker, Peter Lunenfeld, Todd Presner, and Jeffrey Schnapp. 2012. *Digital_Humanities*. Cambridge, MA: MIT Press.

Chan, Anela, Richard Chenhall, Tamara Kohn, and Carolyn Stevens. 2017. "Interdisciplinary Collaboration and Brokerage in the Digital Humanities." *Digital Humanities Quarterly* 11, no. 3.

Clò, Clarissa. 2016. "Inventing the New Renaissance Generation: The Digital Humanities in FL Classroom through Visual Storytelling, Student Curation and Geospatial Scholarship (SWALLT Keynote 2016)." Presented at the Southwest Association for Language Learning Technology, San Diego, April 1. https://drive.google.com/file/d/0Bzh-ABZrF10qVXNsejlOakZ3eDA/view ?usp=sharing&usp=embed_facebook.

Cohen, Cathy. 2016. "Relating Input Factors and Dual Language Proficiency in French–English Bilingual Children." *International Journal of Bilingual Education and Bilingualism* 19, no. 3: 296–313. https://doi.org/10.1080/13670050.2014 .982506.

Cohen, Patricia. 2010. "Digital Keys for Unlocking the Humanities' Riches." *New York Times*, November 16, 2010. https://www.nytimes.com/2010/11/17/arts /17digital.html.

College of Wooster. n.d. "Wiki vs. Blog." Accessed June 17, 2018. https://www .wooster.edu/offices/web/how/scotblogs/wiki-blog/.

Compernolle, Rémi A. van, and Janice McGregor. 2016. *Authenticity, Language and Interaction in Second Language Contexts*. Bristol: Multilingual Matters. https://books.google.com/books?id=5rbQCwAAQBAJ&printsec=frontcover #v=onepage&q&f=false.

Comsa, Maria Teodora. 2017. "Interactive Visualization: Performances of La Partie de Chasse de Henri IV [Created Using Palladio, Http://Hdlab.Stanford.Edu /Palladio]." Mapping the Republic of Letters Data Visualizations. April 2017. http://republicofletters.stanford.edu.

Cordell, Ryan. 2016. "How Not to Teach Digital Humanities." In *Debates in the Digital Humanities*, edited by Matthew K. Gold and Lauren F. Klein. Minneapolis: University of Minnesota Press. http://dhdebates.gc.cuny.edu/debates /text/87.

Cro, Melinda A., and Kiara O'Dea. n.d. "Mapping the Astrée: Character, Geography, and Myth." Mapping the Astrée. Accessed February 11, 2019. https://map pingastree.weebly.com/.

Davidson, Cathy N. 2008. "Humanities 2.0: Promise, Perils, Predictions." *PMLA* 123, no. 3: 707–17.

Davis, Rebecca Frost. 2013. "Digital Pedagogy Keywords." Slideshow presented at the Austin College Digital Humanities Colloquium, February 20. https:// www.slideshare.net/rebeccadavis/digital-pedagogy-keywords.

Davis, Rebecca Frost, Matthew K. Gold, Katherine D. Harris, and Jentery Sayers, eds. 2016. *Digital Pedagogy in the Humanities: Concepts, Models, and Experiments*. MLA Commons. https://digitalpedagogy.mla.hcommons.org/.

De Carlo, Maddalena. 1998. *L'interculturel*. Millau, France: CLE International.

Di Pressi, Haley, Stephanie Gorman, Miriam Posner, Raphael Sasayama, and Tori Schmitt. 2015. "A Student Collaborators' Bill of Rights." Center for Digital Humanities, UCLA. June 8, 2015. http://cdh.ucla.edu/news/a-student -collaborators-bill-of-rights/.

Estill, Laura. 2017. "Collaborative Knowledge Creation and Student-Led Assignment Design: Wikipedia in the University Literature Class." *Digital Humanities Quarterly* 11, no. 3. http://www.digitalhumanities.org/dhq/vol/11/3/000320 /000320.html.

Faith, Ashleigh. 2013. "Coding Skills? Who Needs Coding Skills? A Semi-IT-Phobic Way of Learning Code." *HASTAC* (blog). September 17, 2013. https:// www.hastac.org/blogs/ashleigh-faith/2013/09/17/coding-skills-who-needs -coding-skills-semi-it-phobic-way-learning.

Flanders, Julia. 2009. "The Productive Unease of 21st-Century Digital Scholarship." *Digital Humanities Quarterly* 3, no. 3.

Fried-Booth, Diana L. 2002. *Project Work*. 2nd ed. Oxford: Oxford University Press.

Gardiner, Eileen, and Ronald G. Musto. 2015. *The Digital Humanities: A Primer for Students and Scholars*. New York: Cambridge University Press.

Gass, Susan M., and Larry Selinker. 2008. *Second Language Acquisition: An Introductory Course*. 3rd ed. New York: Routledge.

González-Lloret, Marta. 2016. *A Practical Guide to Integrating Technology into Task-Based Language Teaching*. Digital Shorts. Washington, DC: Georgetown University Press. http://press.georgetown.edu/book/languages/practical-guide -integrating-technology-task-based-language-teaching.

Green, Harriett E. 2016. "Fostering Assessment Strategies for Digital Pedagogy through Faculty–Librarian Collaborations: An Analysis of Student-Generated Multimodal Digital Scholarship." In *Laying the Foundation*, edited by John W. White and Heather Gilbert, 179–204. West Lafayette, IN: Purdue University Press. https://doi.org/10.2307/j.ctt163t7kq.13.

Harris, Katherine D. 2013. "Play, Collaborate, Break, Build, Share: 'Screwing Around' in Digital Pedagogy." *Polymath: An Interdisciplinary Arts and Sciences*

Journal 3, no. 3. https://ojcs.siue.edu/ojs/index.php/polymath/article/view
/2853.

————. n.d. "Triproftri | Researching, Writing, Triathloning." Accessed June 29,
2018. https://triproftri.wordpress.com/.

Heuser, Ryan, Franco Moretti, and Erik Steiner. 2016. "The Emotions of London."
The Stanford Literary Lab Pamphlet Series 13 (October): 1–10.

Hildebrandt, Kristine A., and Shunfu Hu. 2013. "Multimedia Mapping on the
Internet and Language Documentation: New Directions in Interdisciplinarity." *Polymath: An Interdisciplinary Arts and Sciences Journal* 3, no. 3. https://
ojcs.siue.edu/ojs/index.php/polymath/article/view/2842.

Hirsch, Brett D., ed. 2012. *Digital Humanities Pedagogy: Practices, Principles and
Politics.* Open Book Publishers. https://doi.org/10.11647/OBP.0024.

Hockey, Susan. 2004. "The History of Humanities Computing." In *A Companion
to Digital Humanities.* Oxford: Blackwell. http://www.digitalhumanities.org
/companion/view?docId=blackwell/9781405103213/9781405103213.xml&
chunk.id=ss1-2-1&toc.depth=1&toc.id=ss1-2-1&brand=default.

Holden, Christopher L., and Julie M. Sykes. 2011. "Leveraging Mobile Games for
Place-Based Language Learning." *International Journal of Game-Based Learning* 1, no. 2.

Horrigan, John B. 2016. "Digital Readiness Gaps." Pew Research Center. http://
www.pewinternet.org/2016/09/20/digital-readiness-gaps/.

"How Many Hours of Instruction Do Students Need to Reach Intermediate-High
Proficiency?" 2010. Center for Applied Second Language Studies, University
of Oregon. https://casls.uoregon.edu/wp-content/uploads/pdfs/tenquestions
/TBQHoursToReachIH.pdf.

Hu, Shunfu. 2017. "The Manang Languages Project Atlas." The Manang Languages
Project. 2017. https://mananglanguages.isg.siue.edu/atlas/#openModal.

Hunter, E. B. 2016. "Must Humanists Learn to Code? Or: Should I Replace My
Own Carburetor?" *HASTAC* (blog). December 17, 2016. https://www.hastac
.org/blogs/shakespeare-games/2016/12/07/must-humanists-learn-code-or
-should-i-replace-my-own-carburetor.

Kennedy, Kara. 2017. "A Long-Belated Welcome: Accepting Digital Humanities
Methods into Non-DH Classrooms." *Digital Humanities Quarterly* 11, no. 3.

Kirschenbaum, Matthew G. 2010. "What Is Digital Humanities and What's It
Doing in English Departments?" *ADE Bulletin* 150: 55–61.

Kretzschmar, Jr., William A. 2009. "Large-Scale Humanities Computing Projects:
Snakes Eating Tails, or Every End Is a New Beginning?" *Digital Humanities
Quarterly* 3, no. 2.

Kreuger, Cheryl. 2003. "Humanizing Language Courses with Technology, Songs,
and Film." In *Teaching with Technology,* edited by Lara Lomicka and Jessamine
Cooke-Plagwitz, 56–64. Boston: Heinle.

Kuhn, Virginia. 2016. "Multimodal." MLA Commons. *Digital Pedagogy in the Humanities* (blog). https://digitalpedagogy.mla.hcommons.org/keywords /multimodal/.

Larsen-Freeman, Diane, and Marti Anderson. 2011. *Techniques and Principles in Language Teaching.* 3rd ed. Oxford: Oxford University Press.

Leuf, Bo, and Ward Cunningham. 2001. *The Wiki Way: Quick Collaboration on the Web.* Boston: Addison-Wesley Professional.

Liu, Alan. 2012. "Where Is the Cultural Criticism in the Digital Humanities." In *Debates in the Digital Humanities.* Edited by Matthew K. Gold. Minneapolis: University of Minnesota Press. http://dhdebates.gc.cuny.edu/debates /text/20.

Locke, Brandon T. 2017. "Digital Humanities Pedagogy as Essential Liberal Education: A Framework for Curriculum Development." *Digital Humanities Quarterly* 11, no. 3.

Long, Sarah E., Hoyt Bond, and Ted Underwood. 2017. "'Digital' Is Not the Opposite of 'Humanities.'" *The Chronicle of Higher Education*, November 1, 2017. http://www.chronicle.com/article/Digital-Is-Not-the/241634.

Lund, Andreas. 2008. "Wikis: A Collective Approach to Language Production." *ReCALL* 20, no. 1: 35–54. https://doi.org/10.1017/S0958344008000414.

Mahony, Simon, and Elena Pierazzo. 2012. "Teaching Skills or Teaching Methodology?" in Hirsch, *Digital Humanities Pedagogy*, 215–25. Open Book Publishers. https://www.openbookpublishers.com/product.php/161/digital-human ities-pedagogy--practices--principles-and-politics?161/digital-humanities -pedagogy--practices--principles-and-politics.

"Mapping the Republic of Letters." n.d. Accessed June 18, 2018. http://republico fletters.stanford.edu/.

Mauri, Michele, Tommaso Elli, Giorgio Caviglia, Giorgio Uboldi, and Matteo Azzi. 2017. "RAWGraphs: A Visualisation Platform to Create Open Outputs." In *Proceedings of the 12th Biannual Conference on Italian SIGCHI Chapter 17*, 1–5. Cagliari, Italy: ACM Press. https://doi.org/10.1145/3125571 .3125585.

McCandless, David. 2010. "The Beauty of Data Visualization." Presented at the TEDGlobal, Oxford, England, July 2010. https://www.ted.com/talks/david _mccandless_the_beauty_of_data_visualization.

———. n.d. "Information Is Beautiful." Information Is Beautiful. Accessed June 13, 2018. https://informationisbeautiful.net/.

Meyer, Morgan. 2010. "The Rise of the Knowledge Broker." *Science Communication* 32, no. 1: 118–27. https://doi.org/10.1177/1075547009359797.

Moretti, Franco. 2013. *Distant Reading.* 1st ed. London: Verso.

Nance, Kimberly A. 2010. *Teaching Literature in the Languages.* Boston: Prentice Hall.

Pannapacker, William. 2011. "Pannapacker at MLA: Digital Humanities Triumphant?" *The Chronicle of Higher Education Blogs: Brainstorm* (blog). January 8, 2011. http://www.chronicle.com/blogs/brainstorm/pannapacker-at-mla-digital-humanities-triumphant/30915.

Pitman, Thea, and Claire Taylor. 2017. "Where's the ML in DH? And Where's the DH in ML? The Relationship between Modern Languages and Digital Humanities, and an Argument for a Critical DHML." *Digital Humanities Quarterly* 11, no. 1.

Pottroff, Christy. 2015. "New Year's Resolution; or Two Reasons I've Decided to Learn to Code in 2016." *HASTAC* (blog). December 15, 2015. https://www.hastac.org/blogs/cpottroff/2015/12/15/new-years-resolution-or-two-reasons-ive-decided-learn-code-2016.

Prensky, Marc. 2001. "Digital Natives, Digital Immigrants Part 1." *On the Horizon* 9, no. 5: 1–6. https://doi.org/10.1108/10748120110424816.

"Proficiency Targets (Middle School and High School)." 2014. Ohio Department of Education. https://education.ohio.gov/getattachment/Topics/Ohio-s-New-Learning-Standards/Foreign-Language/World-Languages-Model-Curriculum/World-Languages-Model-Curriculum-Framework/Introduction-to-Learning-Standards/Proficiency-and-Research-Based-Proficiency-Targets/Proficiency_target_charts_MCwebsite.pdf.aspx.

"The Programming Historian." n.d. Programming Historian. Accessed February 15, 2019. https://programminghistorian.org/.

Raffa, Guy. n.d. "Danteworlds." Danteworlds. Accessed February 11, 2019. http://danteworlds.laits.utexas.edu/.

Ramsay, Stephen. 2013a. "On Building." In Terras, Nyhan, and Vanhoutte, *Defining Digital Humanities*, 243–45.

———. 2013b. "Who's In and Who's Out." In Terras, Nyhan, and Vanhoutte, *Defining Digital Humanities*, 239–41.

———. 2014. "The Hermeneutics of Screwing Around; or What You Do with a Million Books." In *Pastplay: Teaching and Learning History with Technology*, edited by Kevin Kee, 111–20. Ann Arbor: University of Michigan Press.

Rassaei, Ehsan. 2014. "Scaffolded Feedback, Recasts, and L2 Development: A Sociocultural Perspective." *The Modern Language Journal* 98, no. 1: 417–31.

Reinhardt, Jonathon, and Julie M. Sykes. 2014. "Digital Game and Play Activity in L2 Teaching and Learning." *Language, Learning & Technology* 18, no. 2: 2–8.

Rockwell, Geoffrey. 2013. "Inclusion in the Digital Humanities." In Terras, Nyhan, and Vanhoutte, *Defining Digital Humanities*, 247–53.

Sample, Mark. 2011. "The Digital Humanities Is Not about Building, It's about Sharing." Samplereality. May 25, 2011. http://www.samplereality.com/2011/05/25/the-digital-humanities-is-not-about-building-its-about-sharing/.

Sayers, Jentery. 2011. "Tinker-Centric Pedagogy." In *Collaborative Approaches to the Digital in English Studies*, edited by Laura McGrath, 279–300. Logan,

UT: Computers and Composition Digital Press. http://ccdigitalpress.org/cad/index2.html.

Scholar's Lab. 2016. "Charter." *Scholar's Lab at UVA* (blog). June 2016. http://scholarslab.org/about/charter/.

Shipka, Jody. 2009. "Negotiating Rhetorical, Material, Methodological, and Technological Difference: Evaluating Multimodal Designs." *College Composition and Communication* 61, no. 1.

Sorapure, Madeleine. 2005. "Between Modes: Assessing Student New Media Compositions." *Kairos* 10, no. 2: 1–15.

Spiro, Lisa. 2012. "'This Is Why We Fight': Defining the Values of the Digital Humanities." In *Debates in the Digital Humanities*. Edited by Matthew K. Gold. http://dhdebates.gc.cuny.edu/debates/text/13.

"Strategic Plan." 2018. National Endowment for the Humanities. February 12, 2018. https://www.neh.gov/about/legal/strategic-plan.

Sykes, Julie M. 2011. "Ciberpragmatica 2.0: Nuevos Usos Del Lenguaje En Internet [Cyberpragmatics 2.0: New uses of language on the internet]." *Journal of Pragmatics* 43, no. 10: 2664.

———. 2018. "Digital Games and Language Teaching and Learning." *Foreign Language Annals* 51, no. 1: 219–24. https://doi.org/10.1111/flan.12325.

Tabak, Edin. 2017. "A Hybrid Model for Managing DH Projects." *Digital Humanities Quarterly* 11, no. 1.

Terras, Melissa. 2013. "Peering Inside the Big Tent." In Terras, Nyhan, and Vanhoutte, *Defining Digital Humanities*, 263–70.

Terras, Melissa, Julianne Nyhan, and Edward Vanhoutte, eds. 2013. *Defining Digital Humanities: A Reader*. London: Routledge. https://www.routledge.com/Defining-Digital-Humanities-A-Reader/Terras-Nyhan-Vanhoutte/p/book/9781409469636.

Tschirner, Erwin. 2016. "Listening and Reading Proficiency Levels of College Students." *Foreign Language Annals* 49, no. 2: 201–23. https://doi.org/10.1111/flan.12198.

Underwood, Ted. 2012. "Where to Start with Text Mining." *The Stone and the Shell* (blog). August 14, 2012. https://tedunderwood.com/2012/08/14/where-to-start-with-text-mining/.

———. 2017. "A Genealogy of Distant Reading." *Digital Humanities Quarterly* 11, no. 2.

———. n.d. "The Stone and the Shell." *The Stone and the Shell* (blog). Accessed June 29, 2018. https://tedunderwood.com/.

Unsworth, John. 2002. "What Is Humanities Computing and What Is Not?" *Jahrbuch Für Computerphilologie* 4 (November): 71–84.

Vandendorpe, Christian. 2015. "Wikipedia and the Ecosystem of Knowledge." *Scholarly and Research Communication* 6, no. 3. https://src-online.ca/index.php/src/article/view/201.

Viering, Michaela. 2016. "An Argument for Formative Assessment: Motivation and Persistence." *Pearson Education Blog* (blog). August 1, 2016. https://www .pearsoned.com/formative-assessment-motivation-persistence/.

Vygotsky, Lev. 1978. *Mind in Society: The Development of Higher Psychological Processes.* Cambridge: Harvard University Press.

Weiskott, Eric. 2017. "There Is No Such Thing as 'the Digital Humanities.'" *The Chronicle of Higher Education*, November 1, 2017. http://www.chronicle.com /article/There-Is-No-Such-Thing-as/241633.

White, John W., and Heather Gilbert. 2016. *Laying the Foundation: Digital Humanities in Academic Libraries.* West Lafayette, IN: Purdue University Press.

Whitson, Roger, and Jason Whittaker. 2013. *William Blake and the Digital Humanities.* New York: Routledge.

Williams, George H. 2016. "Access." *Digital Pedagogy in the Humanities: Concepts, Models, and Experiments* (blog). MLA Commons. https://digitalpedagogy.mla .hcommons.org/keywords/access/.

Yancey, Kathleen Blake. 2004. "Looking for Sources of Coherence in a Fragmented World: Notes toward a New Assessment Design." *Computers and Composition* 21, no. 1: 89–102. https://doi.org/10.1016/j.compcom.2003.08.024.

About the Author

Melinda A. Cro is associate professor of French at Kansas State University. She earned her doctorate in Romance Languages (French and Italian) from the University of Georgia in 2010. She has served both as French Language Program Coordinator and Director of Graduate Studies for the Department of Modern Languages at Kansas State and has been responsible for the graduate pedagogy courses in French, including teaching literature and culture in second language acquisition settings. A specialist in early modern literature, pastoral literature, and second language pedagogy and implementing digital humanities in the L2 classroom, her publications include a monograph, *Armas y Letras: la Conquista de Italia (1405–1625)* (2012), and numerous articles appearing in *The French Review, French Studies, Romance Notes, Œuvres et critiques, Studies in Twentieth and Twenty-First Century Literature (STTCL), South Atlantic Review,* and *Moreana.* She currently serves as Contributing Editor for Seventeenth-Century French Studies for *The Year's Work in Modern Language Studies* (Brill).

CPSIA information can be obtained
at www.ICGtesting.com
Printed in the USA
BVHW070337271119
564908BV00002B/9/P